WOODTURNING
EVOLUTION
Dynamic projects for you to make

WOODTURNING
EVOLUTION

Dynamic projects for you to make

NICK AGAR & DAVID SPRINGETT

First published 2011 by
Guild of Master Craftsman Publications Ltd
Castle Place, 166 High Street, Lewes,
East Sussex BN7 1XU

ISBN 978 1 86108 827 7

Publisher Jonathan Bailey
Production Manager Jim Bulley
Managing Editor Gerrie Purcell
Senior Project Editor Dominique Page
Editor Ian Whitelaw
Managing Art Editor Gilda Pacitti
Designer Chloë Alexander
Illustrator Robin Springett

Set in Avant Garde and Frutiger
Colour origination by GMC Reprographics
Printed and bound by Hing Yip Printing Co. Ltd

Dedications

I dedicate this book to my two wonderful children,
Barney and Reuben, who are the best kids a
father could ask for.
Nick Agar

For our granddaughter, Ellie.
David Springett

CONTENTS

Foreword

FOR YEARS I have followed and preached an important turning rule: never let the size of the material drive what you make. But, like anyone that creates objects in and out of wood, I have 'bits and bobs', as Nick Agar terms them, throughout my shop. I wait for that special day when I will find the perfect use for that sacred scrap of burl or the precious chunk of African blackwood that I could not bare to burn. However, if I kept saving every disc, every cut-off or tidbit, soon there would be no room left for me to work. So, periodically I purge my treasures and I give them to friends in need or I use them to keep my family's toes warm on a cold winter's night in Maine. How many times, though, have I put a choice piece back into the treasure chest and saved it from that woodstove fate? Many woodturners know exactly what I am talking about. If only we had some fresh ideas for using those small wooden gems, we might sleep better at night and still be able to move around our studios.

There are many books on woodturning showing us how to create useful, and sometimes useless, objects. This book is somewhat different. It guides us through the creation of various objects that make us think outside the box and help us to see the lathe as the stepping stone to more than just a round creation. From wonderful wall sculpture concepts to bent building boxes and with the inclusion of clear, informative tutorials, there is something here for every woodturning enthusiast.

Woodturning Evolution provides us with an outlet for letting our hair down a bit while still keeping to the tradition of the frugal woodworker. This fun, eclectic mix of form, colour and wit will lead any woodturner on the road to clearing out their scraps with a lifetime of endless projects, and will inspire many new ideas.

Jacques Vesery

Introduction

Although this book has two authors it has been written in the first person singular. Both Nick and David regard this collaboration as an equally shared piece of work so they felt that there should be no distinction.

Nick and I first met at the 2005 Association of Woodturners of Great Britain (AWGB) seminar in Loughborough, England, where we were both demonstrating. I was taken with his innate ability to combine line, form and colour and particularly his unorthodox approach to woodturning. We met again in 2008 at the Irish Woodturners' Guild seminar at Enniscrone, Co. Sligo, Republic of Ireland. It was there that we decided we would like to work together, and the result is this book. I can produce shape and form but I have difficulty seeing beyond the finished form. Nick adds original ways of looking at those forms. He incorporates colour, texture and design, for which I thank him. Working with Nick has taught me so much.

I find it quite exciting seeing ideas develop one stage at a time; and the pieces you see in this book show this slow development step by step. In fact, standing back now, I see the development and it begins to look like a form of segmented turning, in reverse, but with a strange twist. I hope that you, the reader, will find encouragement, inspiration and new ideas within these pages.

David Springett

When David suggested writing a book I was inspired by the proposal. We are so different and the idea of the two of us coming together would seem, to many turners, rather odd. But, I thought the mix of our ideas and approaches would be fresh, as we are such contrasting artists. Maybe it would throw up something new?

After the 25th Anniversary Woodturning Seminar in Ireland in 2008, where we met and talked of the book, we had several meetings to discuss ideas. David was raring to get going while I was caught up with work, so things took time to get under way. When we really got started we realized that the ideas in this book would give many woodturners a nudge into the world of experimentation, and we hoped that it would push them towards new ideas and help to develop new concepts. It was time to make use of those 'boring, little, round, brown bits of wood', stored on shelves that 'you will make something out of one day… maybe'. The ideas we have developed will, hopefully, help turners use some of those 'round, brown bits of wood'.

When writing this book we were constantly coming up with new projects, so we feel that there is still plenty of room for you to explore and develop your own ideas.

Enjoy this book and the ideas within; enjoy the making process, even though it might not always go to plan. I find that if you look at problems as a stimulus rather than a hiccup then those 'happy accidents' will often develop into new ideas.

I have been a professional woodturner for 20 years and it's been an incredible journey that has taken me around the world. In this book I have shared some of the techniques that I have developed and that I use on my own work. I hope that you will be inspired to use some in your own way.

Your only limit is your imagination.

Nick Agar

Suitable Woods

The beauty of the techniques we are about to describe is that they will save you wood and they will save you money, transforming thin plank wood, which is generally less expensive and usually of little use to woodturners, into elegant hollow vessels.

Categories of wood

The woods that we have used for the work produced in this book have been chosen for their distinct properties. These fall into four broad categories:

1 **Pale, bland woods, such as sycamore and maple.** These woods lend themselves to decorative surface treatment as, depending on the pieces chosen, they show little or no differences between their winter and summer growth patterns.

2 **Woods with strong grain patterns, such as zebrano and kingwood.** When using woods with a strong grain pattern, consideration must be given to the finished form of the piece. The grain should enhance the form, not fight with it. In Project 8, Zebrano (see page 86), the strong stripe pattern of the zebrano is used to emphasize the cut and re-assembled form. In the gallery (see page 152) a striking piece of

kingwood has been used to produce a small vessel. Here it creates an interesting 'tunnel' effect on that form, again emphasizing the cutting and re-assembly, but the profile of the finished piece can clearly be seen.

3 **Woods with a marked difference between the density of their dormant winter period and the summer growth, such as ash and oak.** The grain pattern of these woods, when burnt and scrubbed or sandblasted, can create quite a dramatic effect. They add texture and interest without detracting from the overall shape of the finished piece.

4 **Burr woods.** The swirling grain pattern within a burr provides the perfect surface for bronzing techniques. The illusion is created as the surface is transformed from wood to metal and yet the natural wood pattern remains.

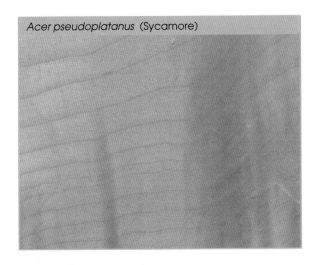
Acer pseudoplatanus (Sycamore)

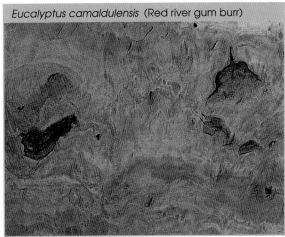
Eucalyptus camaldulensis (Red river gum burr)

Particular woods

Acer pseudoplatanus (Sycamore)

Sycamore is a great wood if it is to be used as a base upon which to apply stains, carved detail, colour, texture and other surface treatments. It holds little attraction as a decorative wood but its clear, creamy colour will allow the form of the turned object to be easily seen. It turns, sands and polishes extremely well.

Acer saccharum (Bird's-eye maple)

A real showy wood with fine pin knots spread throughout the plank. It has a creamy colour and is easy to work as long as the turning tools are sharp. Care must be taken to prevent tearouts that might occur around the small pin knots. It turns, sands and finishes very well, and will accept stain, which when applied skilfully will enhance the completed piece.

Eucalyptus camaldulensis (Red river gum burr)

This burr is ideal for the type of turnery that is described in this book. It is a dense Australian hardwood and, because of its twisted burr grain, it will chip away from the turning tool, leaving a good, clean finish. It has a rich deep red colour and, because of its density, it will finish extremely well.

Fraxinus excelsior (Ash)

Ash is a good, general-purpose wood that is gentle to turn. It is pale cream in colour and has an attractive grain pattern. Occasionally, some ash is quite dense and hard to work, but in general it is a lovely turnery wood.

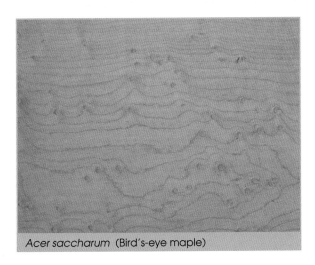
Acer saccharum (Bird's-eye maple)

Fraxinus excelsior (Ash)

Goupia glabra (Kopie)

Microberlinia brazzavillensis (Zebrano)

Goupia glabra (Kopie)

This pale cream coloured wood has little grain pattern and, because it is extremely stable, it is generally used as a furniture substrate beneath veneer. It is a wonderful wood to turn, but not easy to find as it is usually only sold in large quantities. As its grain pattern is so plain it makes an ideal wood to produce base forms upon which any form of decoration may be added.

Ilex aquifolium (Holly)

Holly is a creamy coloured, dense wood that turns exceptionally well. Generally only available in smaller sections, it has been used in this book as a lid for Project 6, the Kiwi vessel (see page 72).

Microberlinia brazzavillensis (Zebrano)

This wood has such a striking grain pattern it is difficult to mistake it for any other. It has a pale buff background with distinct darker brown stripes of varying widths. In Project 8, Zebrano (see page 86) it has been used to make a cut and reassembled vessel in such a way that the stripes in each joined section work against one another to emphasize that joining. It was a surprise to find how well this piece of zebrano worked. Previous experiences have not been so easy.

Swietenia macrophylla (Mahogany and all its various family members)

So often now when confronted with a brown, indistinct, but even-grained wood the temptation is to place it under the general heading of 'Mahogany'. Long gone are the times when rich, dark, dense and highly figured Honduras

Ilex aquifolium (Holly)

Swietenia macrophylla (Mahogany)

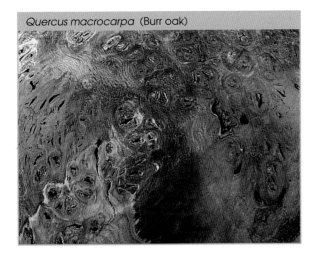
Quercus macrocarpa (Burr oak)

Quercus robur (Oak)

mahogany was easily available, so here the wood that is brown with indistinct but even grain will be given that general heading. The 'mahogany' used here is an easily worked wood and its lack of a strong grain allows it to be turned with very little tearout, making it a useful general-purpose wood upon which to experiment.

Quercus macrocarpa (Burr oak)

The best pieces have remarkable swirling, curly patterns of golden wood that turn beautifully. The interlocking grain can sometimes cause problems, but at least there is not one single area of awkward end grain – it is all over! This is a beautiful wood, and remember that thinner, flat and less expensive pieces may be used for the projects within.

Quercus robur (Oak)

This pale brown wood lends itself to ebonizing – a single coat of vinegar in which wire wool has been steeped will blacken the surface almost immediately. The tannic acid in the oak reacts with the iron causing the surface of the wood to darken.

As there is a clear difference between the summer and winter growth rings, oak lends itself to sand blasting (or burning and wire brushing) to reveal a strongly textured grain pattern.

Oak turns well, but take care to clear the shavings off the tools and the lathe at the end of the working day or the tannic acid will react with the steel of those tools and the lathe bed.

Tools and Equipment

Besides the usual selection of readily available tools that we have used for the projects in this book, there are three that have been made simply by grinding the required shape from high-speed steel. Here we explain how to make them and how to use them, plus list the general tools you'll need.

Square-end tool

This tool, made from ¼ x ¼in (6 x 6mm) high-speed steel, is quite simple to make and very effective to use. The tool is supported on a shelf tool rest when being used **A**.

If you look at the diagram below **1** you will see that the steel has been ground back to produce a cutting angle of about 40° and the sides have been relieved so that they will not bind when a deeper cut is made. Make sure that the wooden handle is long and strong, as this will counteract any downward pressure on the cutting edge.

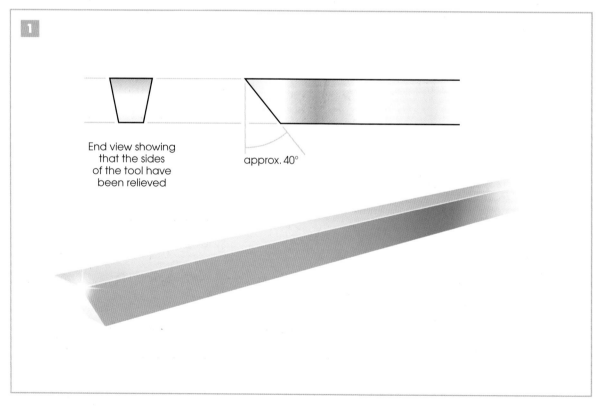

End view showing that the sides of the tool have been relieved

approx. 40°

Slicing tools

These slicing tools are used, supported upon a shelf tool rest, to turn into the work to produce an angled hollow but, with imagination, may have other uses.

The two tools in the foreground **B**, right- and left-handed, have been ground from ⅝ x ¼in (15 x 6mm) high-speed steel. As you can see in the diagram below **2**, the cutting area of both tools is quite short – only about ¼in (6mm) – so that when they are cutting, the chance of 'grab' is reduced. Grinding tools from inexpensive wood chisels is much cheaper than buying commercially produced tools (if they are available). The cost comes in the time that it takes to grind those tools to shape.

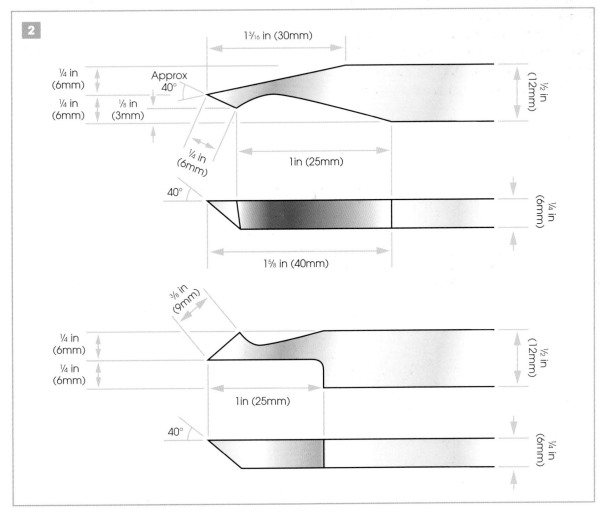

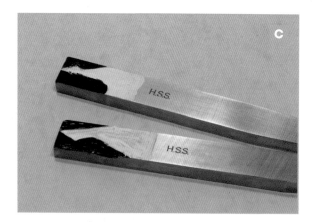

Grinding tools

Before you begin, paint the surface of the steel with typist's correction fluid and, using a pencil, mark the shape to be ground C . Place a bowl of water alongside the grindstone and now patiently grind the steel away towards the pencil line D . Quench regularly to keep the steel cool. Do not be worried about grinding to the precise angles shown in the diagrams; the angles are provided as a guide only. Be relaxed when grinding the shape and the work will proceed much more easily. When complete E , test the tools on a less important piece of wood to ensure that they cut cleanly. Make adjustments where necessary. Producing your own tools can be quite liberating.

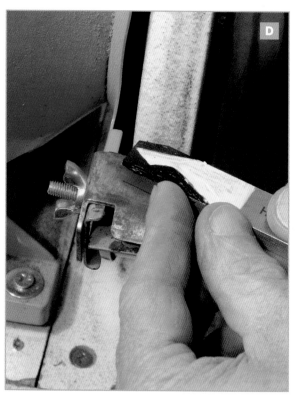

Shelf tool rest

When using the square-end tool and the slicing tools, the shelf tool rest has a considerable advantage over the regular tool rest. If the regular tool rest were to be used to support these tools it could act as a fulcrum and the pressure of the cut could draw the tool down into the work, damaging the cut in progress. When these tools are set flat upon the shelf tool rest (with the tool cutting at centre height) they are fully supported, allowing good control of the cut F . Most turners are accustomed to using a regular tool rest and may initially experience difficulty using the shelf rest. This kind of tool rest requires a different approach, as the tool remains horizontal and firmly flat upon the rest throughout the turning operation.

The points to remember when safely using this unfamiliar support for the tool are:

1 Apply light pressure only on the right hand, which holds the tool handle.

2 Apply firm pressure with the fingers of the left hand to press the tool flat onto the shelf tool rest.

3 Take light cuts with the tool.

A shelf tool rest can easily be made in wood for use in your own tool post **G** . Use a dense hardwood for the shelf. If you like the tool rest and it works for you, then maybe consider buying a more durable steel version.

Basic kit

When turning the projects in this book you will need some or all of the following:

- A captive nut/bolt faceplate with a ⅜in (9mm) bolt and matching nut
- A ⅜in (9mm) drill bit to match the faceplate bolt
- A ⅜in (9mm) gouge
- A ¼in (6mm) square-end tool
- A shelf tool rest
- Card, pencil, rule, protractor and pencil compass

- Thin wood wedges and hammer
- Mallet and chisel
- PVA glue and newspaper
- Hot melt glue gun (optional)
- Yellow glue and masking tape
- Typist's correction fluid
- Small drum sander and flexible drive
- Palm sander (optional)
- C clamps

Any specific additional tools and materials will be listed at the beginning of each project.

When decorating the projects in this book you will need some or all of the following:

- A graphite pencil
- A selection of acrylic paints and brushes
- Pyrograph tool
- A selection of cutting burrs and electric tool on which they fit
- Spray diffuser or pump-action spray bottle
- A selection of coloured spirit stains
- An airbrush and acrylic paints (optional)
- Toothbrush and fine wire brushes
- A selection of cans of coloured automotive sprays or specialist acrylic sprays
- A spray booth or large cardboard box
- Low-tack masking tape (including 2in/50mm width tape)
- Tubes of gold and silver finger wax
- A scalpel
- A set of circle templates or a pencil compass
- Permanent black marker pens
- Vinegar and wire wool
- Propane torch and wire wool
- Vinyl gloves
- Ebonizing spray

Holding the Work

It is advisable that you read and make sure you've entirely understood this section before commencing any of the projects. This will ensure that you are fully prepared, leaving yourself able to concentrate upon the turning methods with which you may be unfamiliar.

Using a captive nut and bolt faceplate

This wood faceplate, with its central bolt screwed into a captive nut on the underside, allows discs of wood with holes at different centres to be held on each of those centres when necessary. Tightening the bolt locks the wood disc firmly against the wood faceplate. The two large surface areas that are tightly pressed together ensure that the wood disc may be turned without slippage. Using this faceplate in conjunction with a newspaper/glue joint (or a hot melt glue weld) provides more freedom and allows the retaining bolt to be removed if necessary.

Occasionally, when repositioning the blank onto the primary centre the blank may run slightly out of true. Don't let this concern you – just loosen the bolt and rotate the blank a small distance clockwise, tighten the bolt and turn the lathe on. If the blank still doesn't run true, repeat the process little by little until it does.

Fitting the captive nut on centre

Select a nut and bolt, about 3in (75mm) long by ⅜in (9mm) diameter.

Cut a wood faceplate disc (the size depends upon size of work to be turned) from plywood or melamine-faced chipboard at least ¹³⁄₁₆in (20mm) thick. Screw the disc centrally to a metal faceplate and turn the edge clean and true. Fix a small (⅛in/3mm) drill bit into a Jacobs chuck held in the tailstock and drill a pilot hole through the wood faceplate **A**.

Remove the metal faceplate (with wood disc attached) from the lathe. Mark a datum on both the metal faceplate and the wood disc. This will ensure that they can be repositioned accurately. Remove the wood disc from the metal faceplate. Measure the distance across the 'points' of the nut, as shown in the diagram on the facing page and select a drill bit of that same size **1**.

Practical Tip

A coach bolt and nut may also be used with the head of the bolt fixed into the underside of the wood faceplate. This is a much quicker method initially but the extended bolt can sometimes interfere with the work.

1   Measure across the points

On the back of the wood disc (the side that touches the metal faceplate), use the selected bit to drill into the wood at the ⅛in (3mm) pilot hole. The depth of the hole must be no more than half the thickness of the wood disc **B**.

Using epoxy resin glue, glue the nut in place, making sure that it is centrally positioned and that it is flat and level **C**.

If the bolt is lightly screwed in place **D** it may be checked, using a try square, to ensure that it is at 90° to the wood surface. Do not leave the bolt in place for there is always the possibility that some of the glue has flowed into the screw thread.

Leave until the glue has set before fixing the wood disc onto the metal faceplate, remembering to align the datum marks.

Test to see if the bolt is running true by screwing it into the captive nut. The bolt should run on centre when the lathe is turned on. If it does not run on centre, remove the bolt and nut and repeat the process until an accurate captive nut and bolt faceplate has been produced.

A large washer is set between the bolt head and the wood blank to spread the load but also, more importantly, to prevent the bolt head digging into the blank's surface.

Drilling centre location holes

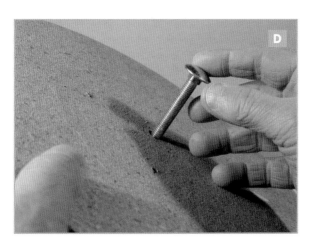

It is vitally important that any centre location holes drilled into the wood blank are drilled at 90° to the face of the work. If these holes are badly drilled then poor work will follow.

In most cases the hole drilled at primary and secondary centres of the blank can be drilled on a pillar drill ensuring that the hole is at 90° to the face of the blank. With larger diameter work the throat of the pillar drill is often not sufficiently deep to allow some points to be reached. In such cases, take an accurately cut smaller block of

wood and mark 'cross hairs' to locate its centre. Continue these lines down the sides and edges using a try square and pencil. This block can be drilled on the pillar drill to ensure that the hole is at 90° to the face of the block.

If the wood blank is marked with cross hairs through both the primary and the secondary point, the drill block can be aligned on either of these points by making sure that the cross hairs on both the block and the wood blank are lined up. The block must be securely held so that a hand drill can be used while the hole in the block accurately guides the bit .

Newspaper/glue joint

This is a much underused method of holding work while turning. The newspaper/glue joint allows work to be held, turned and removed from the lathe without showing any holding marks. The one drawback of this method is that some of the newspaper and glue remains on the surface of the work piece and this will need to be sanded or scraped away.

You should also be aware that if your workshop becomes extremely cold or damp and you use this newspaper/glue holding method, the PVA glue may not dry and this can cause the joint to fail.

Planed or unplaned wood?

When using the newspaper/glue joint it is best to use wood with a planed surface. If, however, you do not own a planer and the wood you have chosen is unplaned do not worry, just make sure that there is sufficient thickness for you to turn both sides. Begin by preparing the blank as described in the particular project – cut the correct diameter, draw the centre line and mark and drill the primary and secondary centres on that centre line as explained. The blank can then be held on the captive nut/bolt faceplate with the bolt through the primary centre and the face of the blank can be turned flat and true F G.

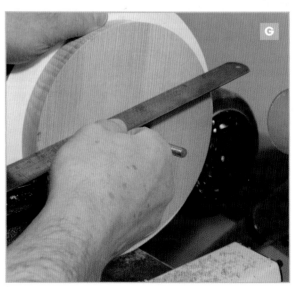

When the piece is removed from the faceplate, the central, unturned circular part that was concealed by the nut can be chiselled or planed flush. The blank can then be remounted, making sure that the planed surface is in contact with the faceplate. Tighten the nut to hold it in place and then repeat the process on the remaining unplaned surface.

The method

The newspaper/glue joint will be used with the central nut and bolt faceplate to ensure that the work piece is held on centre. The bolt also acts as a clamping device. Cut a piece of newspaper a little larger than the blank to be held. At the centre of the piece of newspaper cut a small hole so that the bolt (from the captive nut) can fit through. Spread white PVA glue evenly across the surface of the wood faceplate (not too close to the bolt) and also on the surface of the work piece to be joined (an old credit card, or similar, can be used as a glue spreader) **H**.

Press the newspaper onto the glued wood faceplate, making sure that the hole lines up with the bolt hole. Now place the bolt through the chosen hole (if there are two centres) in the work piece, press the blank in place and then tighten the bolt down. The glue has to dry thoroughly before turning can begin, so it is a good idea to arrange the day's turning schedule so that newspaper/glue joints are put together at the end of the working day, allowing the glue to dry overnight. Be careful if your workshop is unheated, for the glue may not dry thoroughly, especially on wet winter nights.

Once the glue has dried thoroughly, the piece may be turned and the bolt removed (if necessary) at any time, allowing the turning to continue with confidence.

When the turning has been finished, sanded and polished, the newspaper/glue joint may be split from the faceplate. When this joint is split the newspaper shears, leaving half on each side

of the joint line. If fine wood wedges are used to split the joint I then the work will not be damaged.

Removing glued newspaper

The easiest way to remove the newspaper that remains on the wood surface after using a newspaper/glue joint is to scrape the surface. Place the work on a non-slip mat and, using a cabinet scraper or a woodworker's chisel, scrape the surface clean. Use abrasive paper to complete the cleaning.

Hot melt glue weld

This is an alternative holding method to the newspaper/glue joint. Again, the work piece is initially held on a faceplate with a central bolt and captive nut. Once the majority of the turning has been completed and it is time to remove the central bolt, a 'weld' of hot melt glue is applied around the circumference of the work J.

Two points must be considered when applying this hot melt weld. The first is to remember to warm both surfaces to which the glue is applied. This will ensure that the hot glue does not chill and set on contact. If a hot air gun is used (the type used to strip paint, or even a hair drier), the wood surfaces will be sufficiently warmed to ensure that the hot glue grips well. The second point is to make sure that the weld is sufficiently deep to give an adequate grip K.

When the turning is finished, the weld can be picked off the surface and the finished work can be removed.

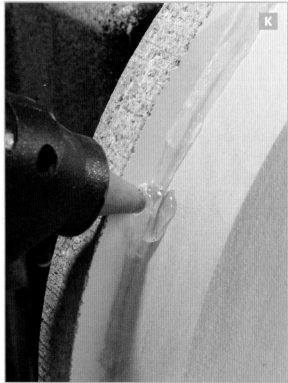

Glues used in the projects

PVA white glue

PVA glue, the white general-purpose wood glue that is used in the UK, is the easiest to use for the newspaper/glue joint. Although this glue is waterproof, when it is used in conjunction with the newspaper to form the temporary fixing, care must be taken not to flood the joint area with liquid (polish, water or thinners), as the newspaper sandwich will take up moisture, become softened and cause the joint to weaken.

Hot melt glue

This glue is applied hot from an electrically heated 'gun' into which the sticks of glue are fitted. The hot, molten glue is squeezed onto the surface that is to be bonded. Warm both surfaces to prevent the hot glue from cooling too rapidly on contact. This temporary bond may be removed by picking the glue from the surface or, if heated gently using a hot air gun, the glue may be softened and removed.

Yellow glue

This glue produces a permanent tight bond between two wood surfaces that have been clamped together. I am assured by turners who produce segmented work that it holds end grain to end grain contact perfectly, and I have found it works extremely well.

Epoxy resin glue

I occasionally use this two-part glue – resin and hardener – for end grain to end grain fixing. If carefully used, securing the joints with masking tape while the glue sets, it provides an excellent bond.

Pictured here are the range of glues that are used in these projects – yellow glue, two-part epoxy resin, hot melt glue and white PVA.

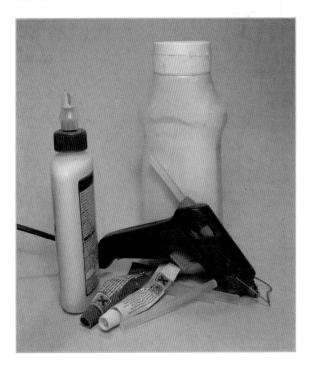

Health and Safety

The projects described in this book are for enjoyment and pleasure. If simple commonsense rules are followed, that pleasure should be a lasting one, so make sure you read these safety points and always take them into account when you're in your workshop.

- Always wear eye protection when turning wood or grinding metal. Always wear a face shield when turning larger pieces of wood.

- Don't forget the vital importance of protecting your lungs from the fine dust that is constantly produced when turning. Various masks are available; the better types filter the air and blow clean, cool air across your face behind a protective visor.

- Keep loose clothing and hair away from the lathe when working.

- If you use a three- or four-jaw metal chuck be aware of those spinning jaws. Before the chuck is used in the lathe, remove the jaws and grind back the sharp external edges. Then if the jaws hit the hand they are more likely to cause a bruise rather than a cut. In addition, paint the ends of the jaws white to make them more visible when the lathe is operating.

- It is good practice to revolve the work by hand to ensure that nothing catches before switching on the lathe.

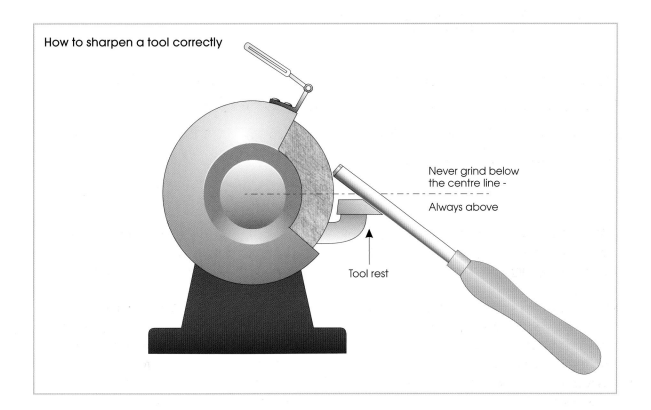

How to sharpen a tool correctly

Never grind below
the centre line -

Always above

Tool rest

- Have the lathe and surrounding area well lit; if a deep cut is being made, use a light that can be moved easily to give the best illumination of the area being worked.

- Do not over-extend the tool when making deep cuts; reposition the tool rest for maximum support.

- Keep all tools sharp. Blunt tools are dangerous because they require more force to produce the cut.

- It is not safe to use a chainsaw without protective clothing that has been specially designed for this purpose. Attending a recognized training course is strongly recommended. Be aware that the regulations governing chainsaw use are revised from time to time; you must keep up to date.

- When using an angle grinder or a similar sculpting tool wear protective clothing and eye protection.

- Do not use woods that might break apart on the lathe. Beware of faults such as dead knots, splits, shakes, loose bark, etc.

- Be aware that some woods can cause skin irritation in some individuals. If this happens, do not use that species again. Barrier creams, latex gloves and dust masks are advisable whenever you are using unfamiliar woods.

- Pay attention to electrical safety and do not allow leads to trail where you, or others, might trip over them.

- Be particularly careful when disposing of any inflammable substances. Wood shavings, finishing materials, oily rags, etc. are all potential fire hazards.

- Do not use a lathe when your concentration is impaired by drugs, alcohol or fatigue.

- Be sensible, take simple precautions, and don't attempt to shortcut them. Enjoy your woodturning in safety.

Finding Inspiration

Besides the general development, or evolution, of ideas within the field of woodturning, most inspiration comes from outside the craft, for if you look inside woodturning you will only repeat what is already being produced. In the search for inspiration, you need to scan a broad horizon.

Form and surface

Take a look at objects in museums and art galleries; look at ceramics, sculpture, micro-organisms, seed pods – in fact any kind of object – and find those that attract you. Consider how that chosen piece, or a part of that piece, might be turned, no matter how impossible it may seem initially. This will cause you to think in different ways and it will jog you out of the rut that you might ordinarily follow.

The same applies to surface decoration. You may not consider yourself artistic but by looking at how other craftsmen (and not necessarily woodturners) decorate their work, or at the textural surfaces of natural and man-made materials, you will find a wealth of possibilities, and in trying to replicate those textures you may develop new ideas.

Today woodturning is dominated by the need to add surface decoration. For years, woodturners did not need to consider the surface decoration of their work, as the beauty of the wood grain was all they needed. On the other hand, the forms that potters created, for instance, were quite plain. Potters therefore needed to enhance the surface, and so they became skilled in that area. The choice for woodturners is a difficult one. Do they choose woods for their spectacular grain and use it as the focal point of their work? Do they cover up beautiful grain just to add decoration? Or do they work with bland woods in the expectation of adding surface decoration? A decision has to be made before work begins, so be clear in your mind which direction you wish to follow with each individual piece of work you undertake.

How the vessels were developed

It began with a discussion on how a regular cross-section (for example, an equal-sided triangle) can be turned on the lathe with that section presented to the rotation of the lathe in different positions...

If the triangle had a line from the point to the centre of the base in line with the centre of rotation then a cone would be turned, as shown in the diagram below **1**. If the triangle were off-set from the lathe centre then a ring with a triangular cross-section would be turned. Each different alignment will then produce different forms.

Now if these pieces are cut radially they will reveal triangular faces that will match one another, as we can see in the diagram on the facing page **2**. One part of a turned form can be seamlessly joined to another part. If the ring, with triangular

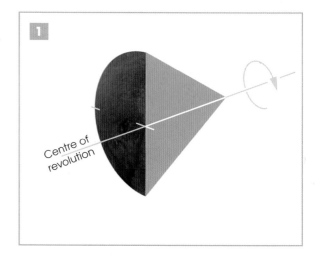

Centre of revolution

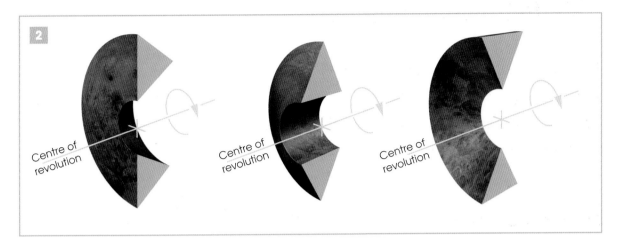

cross-section, is cut into quarters then those quarters, with triangular faces, can be twisted and then reassembled so that the base face of one aligns with the inner face (or outer face) of another **A** . The end faces can be capped with half cones to complete the piece, thus producing a worm-like form **B** . Taking it a little further, we looked at how a Y shape can be turned on different alignments, as seen in the diagram below **3** .

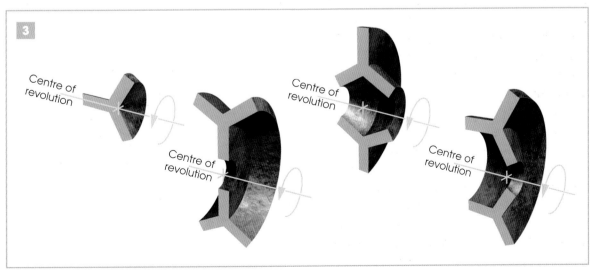

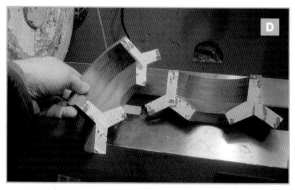

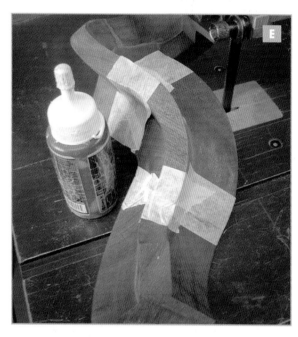

Again, when these pieces are cut, they can be reassembled (as their cross-section is the same) into wonderfully contorted forms. This sequence of photos shows how a Y-shaped form can be turned, cut, reassembled and finished **C** **D** **E** **F**.

Salvador Dali's breakfast bowl

Here is an example of how ideas develop. Having turned the Y form in yew and cut it into four quarter segments, those segments were glued together, as before, to produce a contorted form. The end caps were glued in place but a mistake was made. Instead of arranging the end caps so that the forms' edges flowed in a continuous loop they were set so that they contained a hollow **G**. It was a disappointment at the time but that mistake led onto another idea. Mistakes and problems are an invaluable tool, for they

break the regular thought process and cause the designer to think in a different direction. The change to our thinking that occurred here was that this twisted form, created from a regularly formed cross-section, does not always need to have regular form cross-section. The form that was created looked like an elongated bowl with a very deep foot. LIGHT BULB MOMENT. So why not reduce the foot size and make it more like a simple bowl cross-section? This can then be used as the base form that can be turned on different alignments. In the diagrams **4** **5** we see, first of all, the usual alignment of the bowl cross-section, and then three other (there can be many more if you choose) alignments of the bowl cross-section that can be turned on the lathe. When these have been turned (and yes, it does require a degree of accuracy to turn all to the same cross-sectional

shape), they can be cut into segments. Segments from the various forms can be joined, mixed and matched, and then the ends can be capped with a half bowl section to produce a twisted, almost melted, form of bowl that Salvador Dali, we feel sure, would have been pleased to eat his breakfast from. Below is an artwork of the final piece 6.

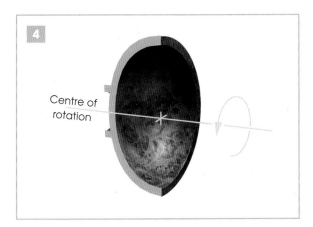

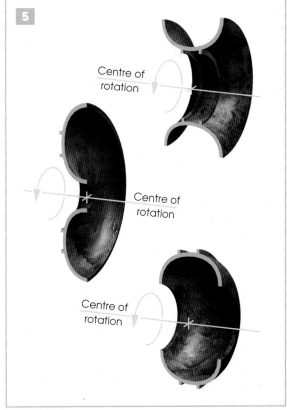

From sculpture to vessel

We realized that these shapes, although very interesting in their own right, had little use except as sculptural forms, so we began to look at a range of hollow forms, particularly square and rectangular hollows H , and how these cross-sections could be presented to the lathe rotation in different positions (similar to the Y) I .

Once these hollow forms had been turned on different axes, they could be cut into parts and, as they had the same cross-section but different curvatures, these different parts could be reassembled into hollow vessels. Add to this mixture the possibility that these hollow forms could be turned eccentrically, and life became very interesting.

But, of course, having decided what we would like to produce we had to find a safe method of production.

Turning these new hollow forms

It then became apparent that a different approach to holding and turning these pieces would be needed. The method used to turn these pieces is quite simple but, like everything

in life, you don't get something for nothing. For this method to work effectively some simple rules need to be followed.

- All surfaces that are required to be turned flat must be dead flat across the diameter (or close to the diameter) of the piece. The edge and inner faces, when required, must be set at 90° to that flat face (or as close as possible).

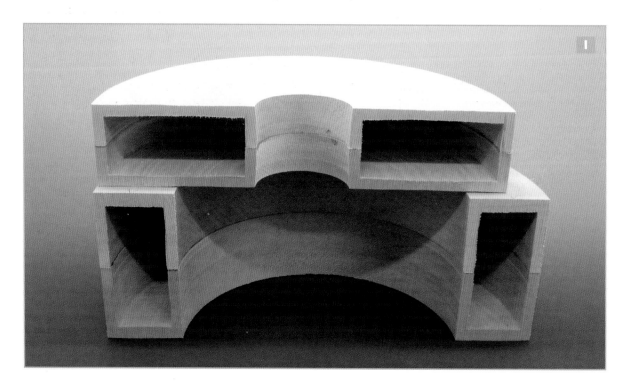

- When the turned parts are cut for reassembly those cuts must be straight, clean and, unless otherwise instructed, at 90° to the face of the work.

- The cuts must be 'radial', i.e. they must run from the centre of rotation to the edge of the work.

- It is important that when a piece is turned with two centre points then only one of these points must be chosen as the centre for the radial cut. It is preferable to use the secondary centre as the location for the start of the radial cut.

- The cut faces must be sanded flat and square by hand with a minimal amount of wood removed.

- Before gluing the segments together, first clean the inside surfaces, which are more easily reached at this point. At this time the inside surfaces may be textured, coloured or further worked if desired.

- When gluing one cut face to another: a) those faces must mate precisely, and b) they must be held firmly together while the glue sets with no slippage and no opening of the glued joint.

- When the glue has dried, the joined surfaces must be cleaned so that the change in curvature from one section to the next is fluid and unnoticeable.

- Dimensions are given for the projects described. If you feel that you would like to make the turned piece larger or smaller, that's fine but please produce a working drawing before you begin, for it will help avoid problems such as discovering that the work will not fit on your lathe.

Cutting costs

One important and valuable benefit of the form of turning described here is the ability to use narrow, relatively thin and generally much cheaper plank wood, which is usually of little

use to woodturners, to produce large hollow vessels. Narrow, thin planks may even be glued edge to edge to make the blank **J** , which is even more cost effective.

Nearly every woodturner has small, relatively thin discs of wood set aside in their wood store waiting to be used but with no use forthcoming. Now there's a way in which they can be used. Rather than turning a thin plate, a tall, elegant vessel can be produced.

Units of measurement

Although care has been taken to ensure that the imperial measurements are true and accurate, they are only conversions from the metric. They have been rounded up or down to the nearest $\frac{1}{32}$in (0.8mm), or to the nearest convenient equivalent in cases where the metric measurements themselves are only approximate and an appearance of greater precision would be misleading.

When following the projects, make sure you use either the metric or the imperial measurements. Do not mix the units. This is because equivalents are not exact. If you choose to work with imperial units it may be advisable to redraw the diagrams to provide precise imperial measurements.

THE PROJECTS

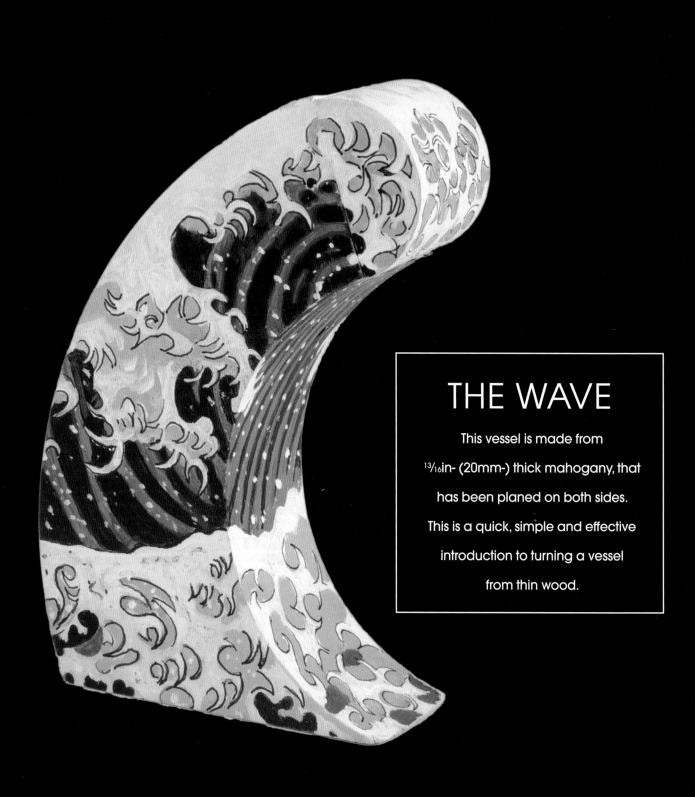

THE WAVE

This vessel is made from
¹³/₁₆in- (20mm-) thick mahogany, that
has been planed on both sides.
This is a quick, simple and effective
introduction to turning a vessel
from thin wood.

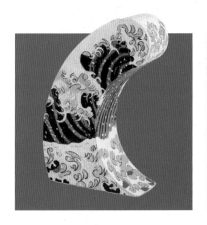

Tools and materials

In addition to the tools and materials shown on page 17, you will need:

- An 8in- (200mm-) diameter piece of $^{13}/_{16}$in- (20mm-) thick mahogany (or similar close-grained wood) that has been planed on both sides
- Two pieces of mahogany $3^3/_{16}$ x 2 x 1in (80 x 50 x 25mm) for the lid

Preparation

1 Take the 8in- (200mm-) diameter blank and draw a centre line, in line with the grain, through the centre point of the cut disc. Mark the centre point (primary point) as X. Measure from point X $^5/_8$in (15mm) along the centre line and mark this as point Y. This will be the secondary centre. At each of these centres, accurately drill a $^3/_8$in (9mm) hole at 90° to the surface of the wood.

2 Fix the blank onto the nut/bolt faceplate with the bolt through the primary centre X. Tighten the nut to hold the work firmly on the faceplate.

Turning the vessel

3 Turn the outer edge clean, true and at 90° to the face of the work.

4 Measure and mark a pencil line $^3/_{16}$in (5mm) from the outer edge and another pencil line $1^3/_8$in (35mm) from that same edge **A**. This will leave a $1^3/_{16}$in (30mm) distance between those pencil lines.

5 On a piece of card mark and cut out a $1^3/_{16}$in- (30mm-) diameter template, as shown **1**.

6 Using a small gouge, turn out a $1^3/_{16}$in- (30mm-) diameter hollow between the marked lines **B**.

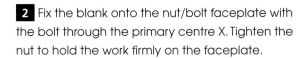

½ in (12mm) $1^3/_{16}$ in (30mm) radius ½ in (12mm)

½ in (12mm)

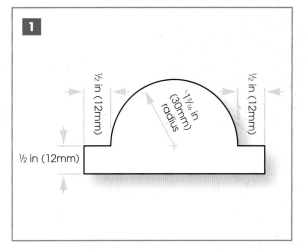

7 Turn from each edge down to the centre, checking regularly with the template **C**. When satisfied, clean up the interior of the hollow taking care not to round over the edges. Polish the hollow but not the edges. The piece may now be removed from the faceplate.

8 The piece is now reversed with the turned hollow facing the faceplate, the bolt is located in the secondary centre Y and, using newspaper and PVA glue, it is fixed to the faceplate **D**. Leave the glue to dry for a least 12 hours before turning. Alternatively a hot melt weld can be applied around the work piece circumference once it is held on centre Y. If the hot melt weld method is used it will allow work to begin immediately.

9 Make sure that the original pencil centre line is still clearly visible. Next rotate the work by hand to bring the centre line horizontal and the shortest part of that line closest to the turner, as shown in the diagram **2**.

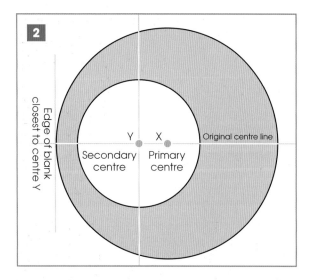

2

Edge of blank closest to centre Y

Y — Secondary centre
X — Primary centre
Original centre line

10 Measure in 1⅝in (40mm) along the centre line towards centre Y. Rotate the lathe by hand and mark a pencil circle with the pencil held at that point **E**. This pencil circle will be offset from the outer edge of the blank.

11 Fit a shelf tool rest in the tool post, to support the square-end tool, making sure that the tool cuts at centre height. Rotate the lathe by hand before turning it on to make sure that nothing catches. Switch on the lathe and, using the square-end tool, turn in on the inner edge (closest to the centre) of the pencil line keeping the tool at 90° to the face of the work **F**.

12 Widen the cut, towards the centre of the work, to prevent the tool from being gripped in the hollow. Continue to turn into the work until the tool reaches the wood faceplate (¹³⁄₁₆in/20mm deep). Widen the opening (towards the centre) enough to allow the inner edge to be sanded smooth. Be careful not to round over the edges. Switch off the lathe and remove the holding bolt **G**.

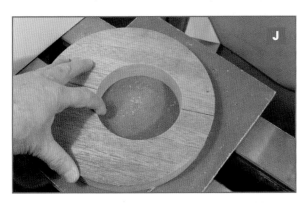

13 Using fine wood wedges split the newspaper/glue joint holding the work to the faceplate **H** . Once the blank has been removed, the newspaper that is still attached to the work **I** , can be sanded off on a firm, flat sheet of abrasive paper. Again avoid rounding over edges **J** .

14 Take the blank to the bandsaw and cut along the marked centre line **K** . Apply yellow glue to the edges and clamp the two halves together aligning those edges perfectly **L** . When you are tightening the clamps, make sure that the glued joint does not slip.

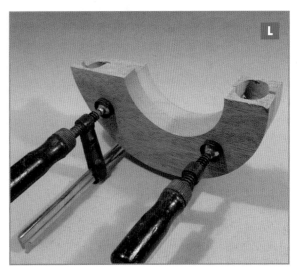

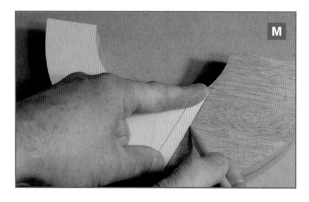

15 To create a more dynamic vessel shape rather than cut into the base of the blank on a radial line, which seems to take all the power out of the shape, first consider the shape shown here **3**. The angle at which the base has been cut (line AB) allows the wave shape to really form itself. To achieve this, cut a template from card and when the glue has dried set the template on the blank and mark along line AB on the template using a pencil **M**. Using a bandsaw, cut along the pencil line AB **N**. The whole piece may now be sanded to a fine finish. The central glue line can be cleaned using a small drum sander.

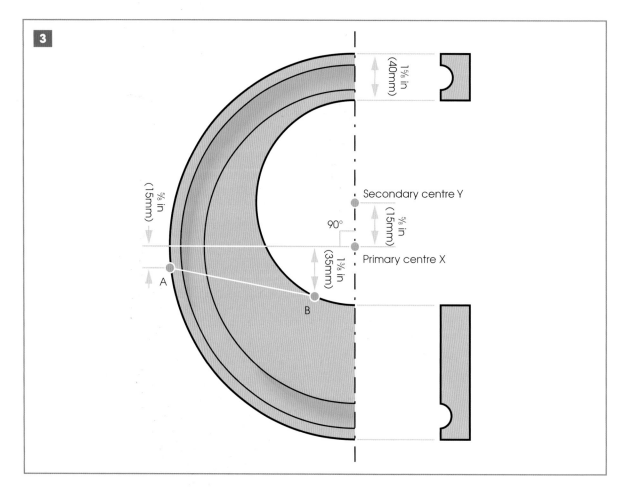

3

1⅝ in (40mm)

⅝ in (15mm)

Secondary centre Y

⅝ in (15mm)

90°

Primary centre X

1⅜ in (35mm)

A

B

Cut-away view of the Wave vessel

Note that the end cap is glued to the turned plug to create a lid.

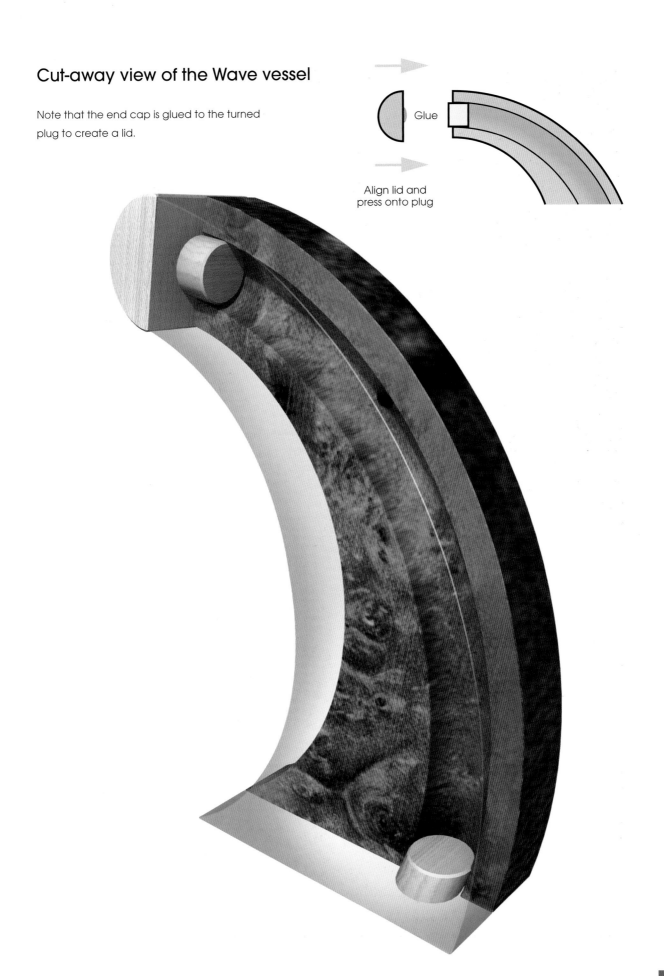

Glue

Align lid and
press onto plug

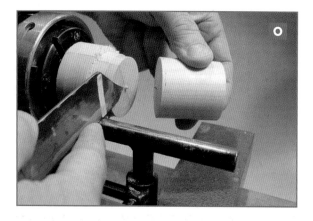

Making the lid

16 Examine the illustration on page 39. From mahogany cut two pieces that are each 3³⁄₁₆ x 2 x 1in (80 x 50 x 25mm). Plane the face of each piece and glue the two faces together using a newspaper/glue joint to produce a blank that is 3³⁄₁₆ x 2 x 2in (80 x 50 x 50mm). Leave overnight to dry. Hold the blank between centres (preferably cup centres that are centred on the glue line) and turn a small spigot on one end, of a size that will fit a small chuck to be held at the headstock. The piece can now be held on the spigot in a chuck, with the tailstock end supported with a cup centre, and this will prevent any possibility of the joint opening.

Measure the end face of the vessel (in this case it is 1⅝in/40mm square) and turn the blank to 1⅝in (40mm) diameter. Withdraw the tailstock and turn the end face of the work flat and true.

Measure 1¾in (45mm) from the end face, towards the headstock, and mark a pencil line. Part off on the headstock side of this line **O** . Set this first piece aside for the moment. Turn the piece remaining in the chuck down so that its diameter is about 1³⁄₁₆in (30mm) diameter. Test this in the hollow end of the vessel so that it is a tight fit. Face off the end of the work and then part off, at 90° to the axis of rotation, a ⅜in (9mm) thick disc. Then turn another which is ⅜in (9mm) long. Let's call these pieces the plugs. Set these plugs aside.

17 Let's return to the lid. This will now be held in a jam chuck so that it can be turned to length. Measure the width of the end of the vessel – in this case it is 1⅝in (40mm) – so measure from the turned end and mark at the unturned end a pencil line this distance from the front. Now, in the chuck, hold a piece of wood that is at least ¹³⁄₁₆in (20mm) larger in diameter than the turned lid blank. Into the face of the work, turn a hole about ¹³⁄₁₆in (20mm) deep and just tight enough to grip the lid blank. If the hole is slightly too large the work can be 'jammed' in using paper kitchen towel that will fill the gap. Make sure that the blank runs true and then turn to the pencil line, facing

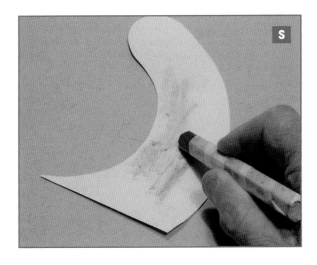

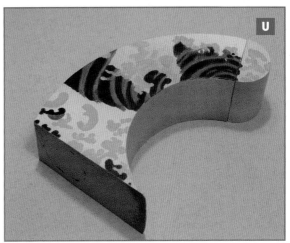

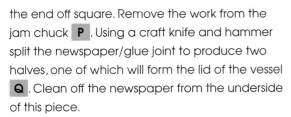

the end off square. Remove the work from the jam chuck **P**. Using a craft knife and hammer split the newspaper/glue joint to produce two halves, one of which will form the lid of the vessel **Q**. Clean off the newspaper from the underside of this piece.

18 As the hollow in the top of the vessel *may* not be precisely on centre, use this method to fit the lid. Place one of the 1³/₁₆in- (30mm-) diameter by ³/₈in- (9mm-) long plugs into the hollow end of the vessel with at least half sticking out. If you are afraid that it will disappear inside then use some kitchen towel in the hollow to make the fit tight. Next lay the vessel on its side on the work bench. Squeeze a little yellow glue onto the end of the plug and then bring the semicircular lid top, flat face, towards the plug. Gently rub the lid on the glued surface of the plug and it will begin to grip. Align all edges of the lid with the vessel and when satisfied leave to dry. When the glue has set the lid can be removed. The second plug is used to fill the hollow in the base. Glue it in and when dry sand off cleanly.

Colouring the vessel

19 This piece has been decorated with Hokusai's well known 'The Great Wave off Kanagawa'. This Japanese woodblock print was first produced in about 1831 and it just seemed to fit the shape. It could be airbrushed on but not all turners have airbrushes, so it was decide to paint the great wave **R**. As it is a wood block print the areas of

colour are well defined, and this makes it relatively easy to paint. A computer has been used to bend the wave print onto a scanned template of the vessel. A graphite pencil is then rubbed on the back of the template **S** to allow an outline of the wave to be traced onto the vessel's surface **T**.

20 Using Prussian blue and white acrylic paint, areas of colour are simply blocked in **U**. It looks a little crude to begin with but as each colour is applied it becomes more refined. It is surprising how easy it is. The blue and white are mixed and the colour can be checked against the print. When the blocked-in colours are dry, use a fine-line black marker pen to draw in the fine detail. If you are not happy at any stage it is quite easy to sand off the area and start again. Like all things, the technique will improve with practice and understanding. The top surface has a sea blue sponge decorative finish and the underside of the wave is developed from the wave decoration on either side.

'CHINESE' VESSEL

This vessel is turned from two fairly thin, relatively small pieces of wood that have been edge joined to form the base blank, making this quite an economical production method. The technique is an extension of the method shown in the previous project.

Tools and materials

In addition to the tools and materials shown on page 17 you will need:

- Two good, flat pieces of hardwood (here English ash is used) planed all round. They are each 8⅜ x 4³⁄₁₆ x ¹³⁄₁₆in (210 x 105 x 20mm). They are glued edge to edge to produce an 8⅜in (210mm) square blank
- Ball end and cylindrical burrs

Preparation

1 As the blank has been glued together, the glue line will also act as the centre line of the blank. If a single piece of wood is being used then mark a clear, matching pencil centre line on both sides of the blank. Mark the centre point of this line and label it X, the primary centre. Measure ⅝in (15mm) from point X along the centre line to locate the secondary centre Y.

Set a pair of pencil compasses to 4³⁄₁₆in (105mm) radius and, with the compass point on primary centre X, draw a circle. Cut the circular blank on the bandsaw.

At the primary centre X and the secondary centre Y drill a ⅜in (9mm) hole, making sure that these are drilled at 90° to the face of the work.

Fit the captive nut/bolt faceplate at the headstock (here we have used the coach bolt faceplate). Take the circular blank and, at the primary centre X, fit the bolt through the prepared hole. Tighten the blank onto the faceplate.

Turning the vessel

2 Even when planed wood is used, occasionally the surface will need to be skimmed. If this is the case it is necessary to check that the finished surface is flat and true **A**. Turn the edge clean to 8in (200mm) diameter, true and square to the top face **B**. One of the good points of this form of turning is that the diameter of the blank does not have to be turned to a precise dimension, for measurements are taken from the turned outer

edge whatever the diameter of that edge might be. Here, as drawings and templates are provided with dimensions, it is sensible to be as close to the 8in (200mm) suggested diameter as possible.

3 From the outer edge, measure along the centre line (the joint line of the prepared blank), first ³⁄₁₆in (5mm), marking it as line 1, followed by ¹³⁄₁₆in (20mm) from the edge, marking it as line 2,

then 1in (25mm), again from the edge, and mark that as line 3. With the lathe rotating mark pencil lines at these positions **C**.

4 Take the square-end tool and, using typist correction fluid, mark a point ⅝in (15mm) from the cutting edge on the top surface of the tool **D**. If the square-end tool were to be used with the regular tool rest there is the possibility of it being drawn into the work, as the rest can act as a fulcrum. This is more likely to happen as deeper cuts are made. To prevent this, a shelf tool rest is used, as this supports the tool more effectively. Set the square-end tool on the shelf tool rest so that it cuts at centre height and begin cutting between lines 1 and 2 to the ⅝in (15mm) marked depth on the tool **E**.

5 Make sure that the base of the hollow is flat and clean. The hollow may now be sanded but do not round over any of the edges. The piece can now be removed from the faceplate and repositioned with the bolt through the secondary centre Y. The blank is now set eccentrically on the faceplate with the turned hollow facing out **F**.

6 A ⅝in- (15mm-) wide by ⅝in- (15mm-) deep hollow will now be turned again. Measure along the centre line to the new centre of rotation Y. On one side it will measure 4½in (115mm) to the edge and on the other 3⅜in (85mm) to the edge. Set the blank so that the centre line is horizontal and the smaller measurement to centre Y is closest to the turner. Place a pencil on line 1 and rotate the lathe by hand to draw the new pathway of line 1. With the blank arranged, again, with the smaller measurement to centre Y closest to the turner, set the pencil on line 2. Rotate the lathe by hand to draw the new pathway of line 2. It will be noticed that the new pathway coincides with the old at one position **G**. This new pathway, between lines 1 and 2, needs to be turned out to a depth of ⅝in (15mm) **H** **I**.

7 The first part is now complete and the blank can be removed from the faceplate. The unturned crescent of wood that remains between the two

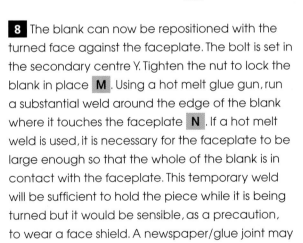

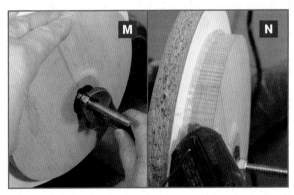

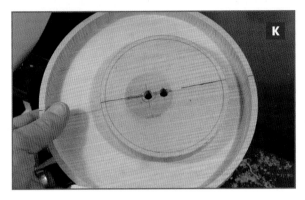

hollows can be removed using a wood chisel and mallet **J** **K** If, having skimmed the surface of the blank, there remains a raised area around the bolt holes this will need to be removed to ensure that the face is completely flat **L**.

8 The blank can now be repositioned with the turned face against the faceplate. The bolt is set in the secondary centre Y. Tighten the nut to lock the blank in place **M**. Using a hot melt glue gun, run a substantial weld around the edge of the blank where it touches the faceplate **N**. If a hot melt weld is used, it is necessary for the faceplate to be large enough so that the whole of the blank is in contact with the faceplate. This temporary weld will be sufficient to hold the piece while it is being turned but it would be sensible, as a precaution, to wear a face shield. A newspaper/glue joint may be used instead of the hot melt weld if desired.

9 Position the blank so that the centre line is horizontal and the shorter of the measurements to the centre Y – approximately 3⅜in (85mm) – is closest to the turner. Measure along the nearest centre line, from the edge inwards, 1in (25mm).

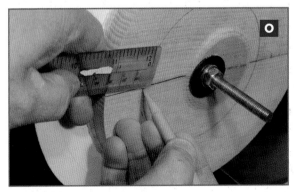

Rotating the lathe by hand, mark a pencil circle from this point **O**. It is always a good idea to rotate the lathe by hand before starting to turn

to ensure that nothing catches. Using the square-end tool, supported on the shelf tool rest and set at centre height, cut on the centre side of the line at 90° to the face of the work. Continue with light cuts and widen the groove so that the tool will not bind. Turn in until the tool touches the wood faceplate P .

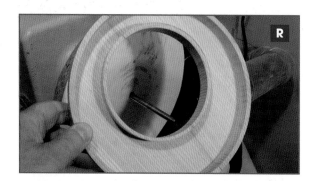

10 Remove the bolt and the centre waste piece. Thoroughly clean up the inside face. When satisfied, carefully pick off the glue weld Q and remove the finished blank R . Take the blank to the bandsaw and cut through the centre line, producing two identical, but mirrored halves S . These two halves may be glued together using yellow glue to form a curved hollow that tapers from small to large T . When the glue has dried, clean up the blank, which can now be cut to produce the basis of two vessels.

11 The blank is marked out according to the details shown in the diagram on the facing page 1 . The first cut is made on line AB, and the piece above this line will be used for the 'Chinese' vessel. If a second cut is made on line CD, the larger, remaining piece will be used for the 'Clarice Cliff' vessel (see the next project). Having marked the lines, set the piece on the bandsaw and carefully cut through on the marked positions U . Now carefully sand clean the top and base cuts of each vessel.

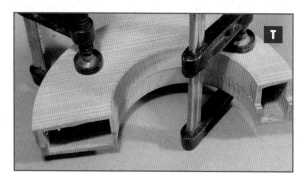

12 The method of fitting the base will be exactly the same for all vessels made this way. Either measure the opening of the base or trace the opening V . Cut a ¼in- (6mm-) thick piece of

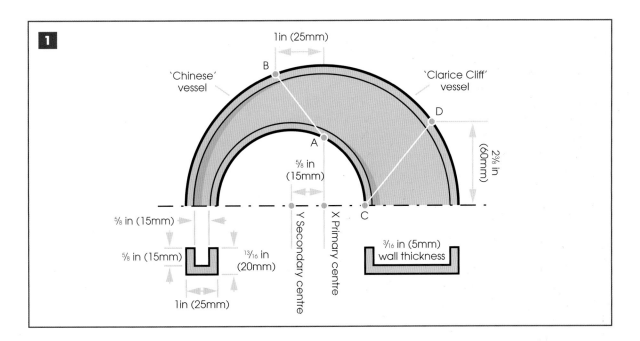

1

'Chinese' vessel

'Clarice Cliff' vessel

1in (25mm)

B

D

A

2⅜ in (60mm)

⅝ in (15mm)

Y Secondary centre

X Primary centre

C

⅝ in (15mm)

⅝ in (15mm)

¹³⁄₁₆ in (20mm)

1in (25mm)

³⁄₁₆ in (5mm) wall thickness

matching wood the size of the base opening. Test in place and adjust where necessary. Place the base on polythene and apply glue to its edges **W** . Press the vessel onto the glued base, leave until the glue has set and then clean the base **X** .

Making the lid and finial

13 For the lid of this 'Chinese' vessel, select or cut a piece of ¼in- (6mm-) thick wood and plane both sides. Measure the top of the vessel – in this case 1⅝in (40mm) by 1in (25mm) – and cut to that size. Mark pencil lines diagonally between the corners to locate the centre. To make the interior of the lid, start by measuring the interior of the vessel (1³⁄₁₆in/30mm by ⅝in/15mm). Cut a ¼in- (6mm-) thick piece of wood to that size and clean the edges, checking that it is a good fit. Set these two pieces to one side while the finial is turned.

14 The finial is just a basic piece of spindle turning. Take a piece of wood (here it is ash) 1³⁄₁₆in (30mm) square by approximately 2¹³⁄₁₆in (70mm) long. Turn the blank round, between centres, with a spigot at the tailstock end. This spigot should be of a size that will fit comfortably, and be held firmly, in a chuck to be fitted at the headstock. Remove the turned blank. Fit the chuck on the lathe headstock and the turned spigot of the blank into that chuck. Bring the revolving centre forward to support the

V

W

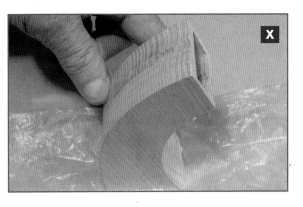

X

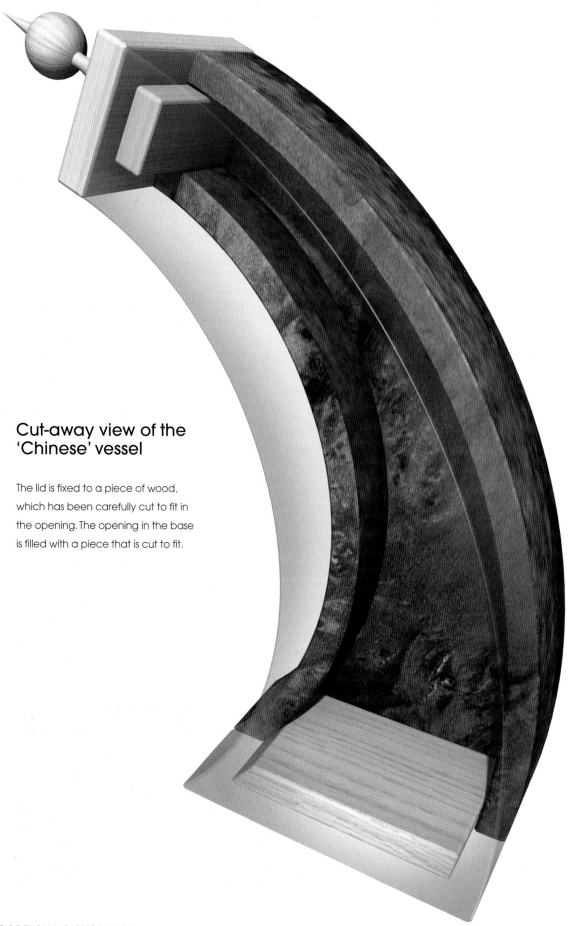

Cut-away view of the 'Chinese' vessel

The lid is fixed to a piece of wood, which has been carefully cut to fit in the opening. The opening in the base is filled with a piece that is cut to fit.

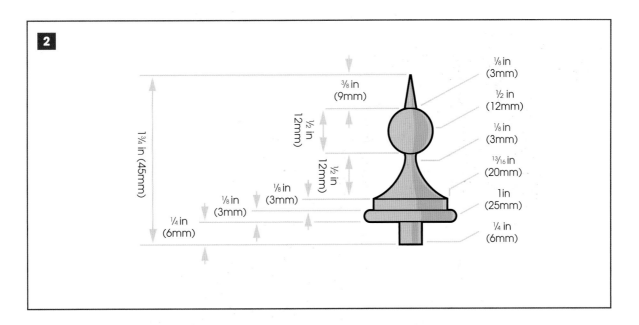

2

⅛ in (3mm)

½ in (12mm)

⅜ in (9mm)

½ in (12mm)

½ in (12mm)

⅛ in (3mm)

1¾ in (45mm)

⅛ in (3mm)

⅛ in (3mm)

¼ in (6mm)

⅛ in (3mm)

½ in (12mm)

⅛ in (3mm)

¹³/₁₆ in (20mm)

1 in (25mm)

¼ in (6mm)

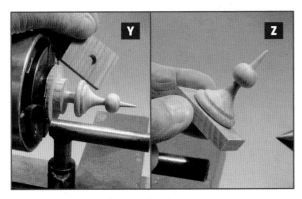

end of the blank. Next turn the blank to a clean 1in (25mm) diameter. Following the dimensions shown in the diagram above **2**, first turn the ½in- (12mm-) diameter ball close to the end of the finial. Next turn the ⅛in- (3mm-) wide, ¹³/₁₆in- (20mm-) diameter step. This step is approximately ½in (12mm) away from the end of the ball measured towards the headstock. Using a fine gouge, make a sweeping cut from the edge of that step down towards the turned ball. The diameter at the junction of the ball shape and the sweeping cut will be about ⅛in (3mm). On the headstock side of the marked 'collar' initially turn down to about ½in (12mm). Carefully round over the edges of the collar. The point at the tailstock end of the finial may now be turned, so turn the area on the tailstock side of the ball to ⅛in (3mm), slicing away from that position so that it tapers, and is parted off, to a point ⅜in (9mm) away.

Clean up the piece but do not polish. Finally turn, on the headstock side of the collar, down to ¼in (6mm) and part it off to leave a ¼in- (6mm-) long spigot.

15 Take the lid prepared earlier (approximate size 1⅝ x 1 x ¼in/40 x 25 x 6mm) and at the marked centre drill a ¼in (6mm) hole **Y**. Glue the finial to the lid **Z** and when the glue has dried clean off the underside, making sure that the base is clean and flush. Take the prepared lid interior, which is 1³/₁₆ x ⅝ x ¼in (30 x 15 x 6mm). On the underside of the lid top centrally mark the lid interior sizes. Carefully glue the lid interior to the underside of the lid, making sure that it is centrally aligned on the marks. Leave until the glue is dry, then check the fit and make adjustments where necessary **A1**. To ensure that the lid will stay in place, use small pill magnets on the lid interior edge and the inside of the vessel **B1**.

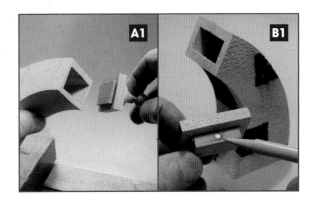

Design Alternative

The Pigtail Lid

This alternative design for the lid **C1** goes perfectly with the 'Chinese' vessel. Thanks go to turner Allan Beecham for explaining this technique which, over the past few years, has been mangled into the form described here.

16 Start by choosing a good close-grained hardwood. This is essential if a successful pigtail is to be produced. Here lemonwood is used. Prepare the blank as described earlier when turning the finial – same sizes, same approach, holding the blank in the chuck and supporting the tailstock end with a revolving centre. Turn the blank to ⅞in (22mm) diameter and mark out, in pencil, all the important points, following the diagram shown here **3** . Turn from the collar and slope down towards the start of the curve of the 'flame' shape. It should be about ⅜in (9mm) diameter at this point. This slope and the curve of the 'flame' shape are turned, little by little, together. Complete the 'flame' shape and part off at the tailstock end. On the headstock side of the collar turn down to about ½in (12mm) **D1** .

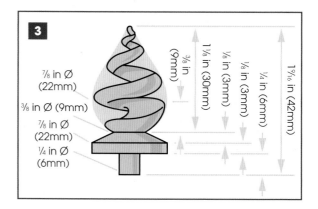

17 Divide the flame shape into a series of regular divisions along its length. Here there are eight lines. Next draw four horizontal lines, the first at 12 o'clock, the second at 3 o'clock, the third at 6 o'clock and the fourth at 9 o'clock, as shown in the diagram **4** . Now, using a pencil, join points 1A to 2C, 2C to 3A, 3A to 4C, 4C to 5A, 5A to 6B, 6B to 7C and 7C to 8D. It will be noted that towards the tip of the flame the spiral speeds up **E1** .

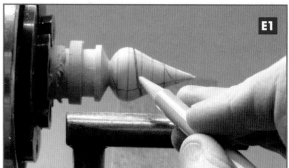

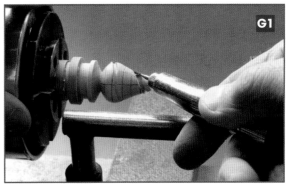

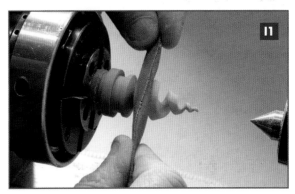

18 Using a junior hacksaw, with the teeth facing backwards so that the cut is less aggressive, follow that spiral line **F1**. Use a series of burrs, held in a flexible drive or similar, to carve that spiral line **G1** **H1**. The carved spiral groove has to be cut deeply, going beyond half the thickness of the flame shape to produce the open twist. Work from the point of the pigtail towards the heavier, bulky end, as the point of the pigtail will become very fragile. Complete the piece with careful hand sanding **I1** **J1** **K1**. Turn on the lathe and on the headstock side of the collar turn down to ¼in (6mm) diameter and part off leaving a ¼in- (6mm) long spigot attached to the pigtail.

The pigtail was sprayed black to complement the decorative black square patterning on the green vessel. Fit the pigtail to the lid as described earlier (see page 49), remembering to use magnets to ensure that the lid is held firmly in place.

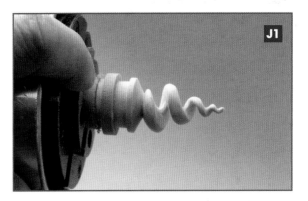

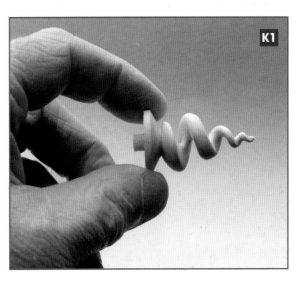

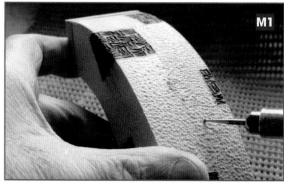

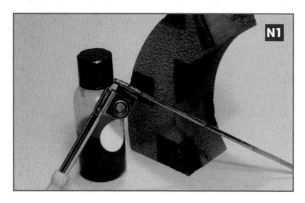

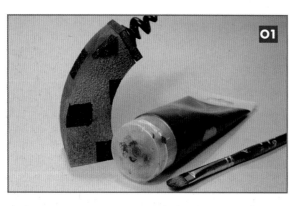

Decorating the vessels

19 In both cases the dark square, or round, areas have been worked with a poker pen. The square areas have been branded using the poker pen with its wire tip bent into a multiple Z form. Before branding the squares, mask the areas to be left plain using masking tape. This will prevent the soot from the burnt areas discolouring the surrounding wood **L1**. Once all the chosen areas have been burnt, use a fine wire brush to remove all the loose burnt dust. Remove the masking tape and using a spherical burr, in a flexible drive, texture the surface between the burnt squares **M1**.

Some points to consider when texturing:

- Try to apply the burr randomly, as the eye will notice straight lines.

- Be deliberate in applying the burr. A tentative approach will not produce good texturing.

- Be careful at the edges of the work, for the burr can easily 'drop over' that edge and cause an unsightly cut.

- Finish one whole side before taking a break, because hand pressure can be different and a line will show in the texturing.

- End grain is more resistant than side grain. Try to compensate.

- Clean the textured area using a fine brass wire brush or soft plastic rotary brushes, as steel wire brushes can discolour the wood.

20 Use a spirit stain and diffuser to colour the whole vessel. Here red dye was used on the vessel with circular patterns, and green for the vessel with square patterning **N1**. Leave until dry, and then mask the areas around the burnt patterning so that they may be darkened using black acrylic paint. Leave until dry and remove the masking tape **O1**. Apply several coats of clear lacquer. When the lacquer is dry the black square can be 'lifted' slightly by applying a gold wax that is brushed in and brushed off using a tooth brush **P1**. When completely satisfied glue the black pigtail into the lid top. The red vessel's black areas have not been enhanced.

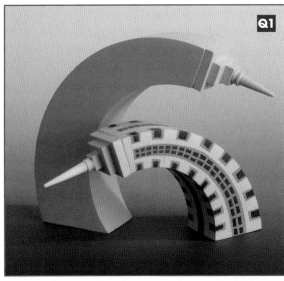

Bendy skyscrapers

These are just fun extensions of the same turning method, but the basic hollow blank is left uncut as one whole piece **Q1**. As the top (lid) of the building extends far from the base this vessel can tip over, so before the base is glued in place a counter weight is glued inside **R1**.

Here the form has been sprayed with a base colour **S1** and the area masked off with masking tape. The window sections are cut away **T1** and the piece is sprayed with a second colour **U1**, followed by window details being drawn or airbrushed in.

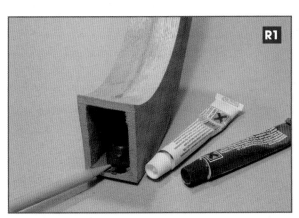

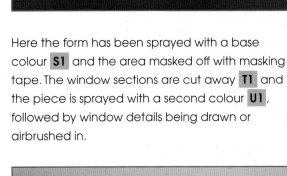

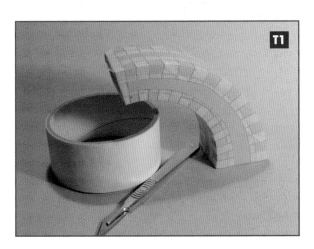

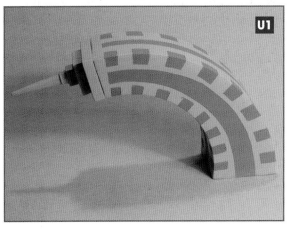

'CLARICE CLIFF' VESSEL

More substantial than the 'Chinese' vessel, this piece provides a larger surface

that can be airbrushed (or hand painted) with an Art Deco design

based upon the work of Clarice Cliff.

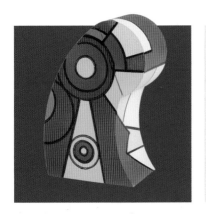

Tools and materials

In addition to the tools and materials shown on page 17 you will need:

- Two good, flat pieces of hardwood (here English ash is used) planed all round. They are each 8⅜ x 4³⁄₁₆ x ¹³⁄₁₆ in (210 x 105 x 20mm). They are glued edge to edge to produce an 8⅜in (210mm) square blank

Art Deco inspiration

Clarice Cliff was a English designer of ceramics in the Staffordshire Potteries from the 1920s onwards, and she produced a startling range of brilliantly coloured Art Deco pieces that are highly collectable today. Just search her name on the Internet to see the inspirational designs. The vessel in this project is based upon the same turning operation as the 'Chinese' vessel in the previous project, so if you have completed that project you will have the basic vessel for this one and you can skip to step 11. If not, then follow the steps below.

Preparation

1 As the blank has been glued together, the glue line will also act as the centre line of the blank. If a single piece of wood is being used then mark a clear, matching pencil centre line on both sides of the blank. Mark the centre point of this line and label it X, the primary centre. Measure ⅝in (15mm) from point X along the centre line to locate the secondary centre Y.

Set a pair of pencil compasses to 4³⁄₁₆in (105mm) radius and, with the compass point on primary centre X, draw a circle. Cut the circular blank on the bandsaw.

At the primary centre X and the secondary centre Y drill a ⅜in (9mm) hole, making sure that these are drilled at 90° to the face of the work.

Now fit the captive nut/bolt faceplate at the headstock (in this case we have used the coach bolt faceplate). Take the circular blank

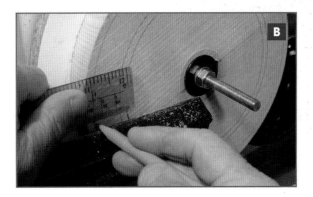

and, at the primary centre X, fit the bolt through the prepared hole. Tighten the blank onto the faceplate.

Turning the vessel

2 Turn the edge clean to 8in (200mm) diameter, true and square to the top face **A** . From the outer edge, measure along the centre line, (the joint line of the prepared blank), first ³⁄₁₆in (5mm), marking it as line 1, followed by ¹³⁄₁₆in (20mm) from the edge, marking it as line 2, then 1in (25mm), again from the edge, and mark that as line 3. With the lathe rotating, mark pencil lines at these positions **B** .

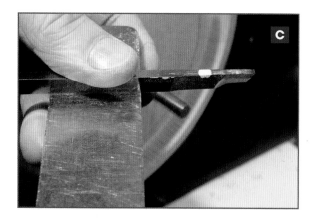

3 Take the square-end tool and, using typist correction fluid, mark a point ⅝in (15mm) from the cutting edge on the top surface of the tool . A shelf tool rest is used to support the square-end tool as this will prevent the tool from being drawn into the work. Set the square-end tool on the shelf tool rest so that it cuts at centre height and begin cutting between lines 1 and 2 to the ⅝in (15mm) marked depth on the tool **D**.

4 Make sure that the base of the hollow is flat and clean. The hollow may now be sanded but do not round over any of the edges. The piece can now be removed from the faceplate and repositioned with the bolt through the secondary centre Y. The blank is now set eccentrically on the faceplate with the turned hollow facing out **E**.

5 A ⅝in- (15mm-) wide by ⅝in- (15mm-) deep hollow will now be turned again. Measure along the centre line to the new centre of rotation Y. On one side it will measure 4½in (115mm) to the edge and on the other 3⅜in (85mm) to the edge. Set the blank so that the centre line is horizontal and the smaller measurement to centre Y is closest to the turner. Place a pencil on line 1 and rotate the lathe by hand to draw the new pathway of line 1. With the blank arranged, again, with the smaller measurement to centre Y closest to the turner, set the pencil on line 2. Rotate the lathe by hand to draw the new pathway of line 2. It will be noticed that the new pathway coincides with the old at one position **F**. This new pathway, between lines 1 and 2, needs to be turned out to a depth of ⅝in (15mm) **G** **H**.

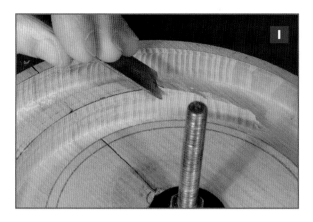

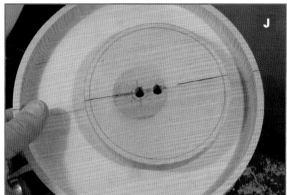

6 The first part is now complete and the blank can be removed from the faceplate. The unturned crescent of wood that remains between the two hollows can be removed using a wood chisel and mallet **I** . If, having skimmed the surface of the blank, there remains a raised area around the bolt holes this will need to be removed to ensure that the face is completely flat **J** .

7 The blank can now be repositioned with the turned face against the faceplate. The bolt is set in the secondary centre Y. Tighten the nut to lock the blank in place **K** . Using a hot melt glue gun, run a substantial weld around the edge of the blank where it touches the faceplate **L** . If a hot melt weld is used, it is necessary for the faceplate to be large enough so that the whole of the blank is in contact with the faceplate. This temporary weld will be sufficient to hold the piece while it is being turned but it would be sensible, as a precaution, to wear a face shield. A newspaper/glue joint may be used instead of the hot melt weld if desired.

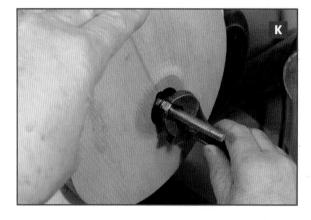

8 Position the blank so that the centre line is horizontal and the shorter of the measurements to the centre Y – approximately 3⅜in (85mm) – is closest to the turner. Measure along the nearest centre line, from the edge inwards, 1in (25mm). Rotating the lathe by hand, mark a pencil circle from this point **M** . It is always a good idea to rotate the lathe by hand before starting to turn to ensure that nothing catches. Using the square-end tool, supported on the shelf tool rest and set at centre height, cut on the centre side of the line at 90° to the face of the work. Continue with light

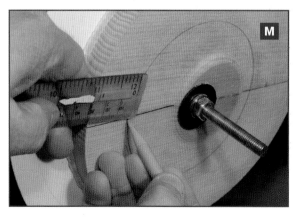

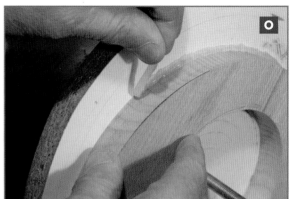

cuts and widen the groove so that the tool will not bind. Turn in until the tool touches the wood faceplate 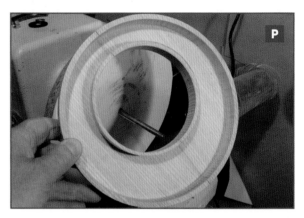N.

9 Remove the bolt and the centre waste piece. Thoroughly clean up the inside face and, when satisfied, carefully pick off the glue weld **O** and remove the finished blank **P**. Take the blank to the bandsaw and cut through the centre line, producing two identical, but mirrored halves **Q**. These two halves may be glued together using yellow glue to form a curved hollow that tapers from small to large **R**.

10 When the glue has dried, clean up the blank, which can now be cut to produce the 'Clarice Cliff' vessel. Mark the blank out following the details in the diagram on page 60 **1**. The first cut is made on line AB. The second cut is made on line CD. The vessel is the section between these two lines. (The top section is used to make the 'Chinese' vessel in the previous project.)

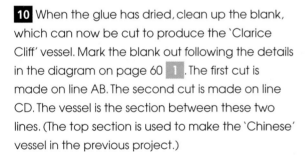

The lid of this vessel, made in a similar manner to the Wave vessel on page 40, will have to fit the larger top and so will be produced from a split cylinder approximately 2in (50mm) in diameter. It will be glued to a ¼in- (6mm-) thick piece of wood that will be cut to match the vessel's opening. The base of the vessel is made and fitted as described when making the 'Chinese' vessel on page 46.

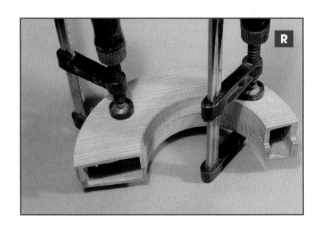

Cut-away view of the 'Clarice Cliff' vessel

Note how the lid is fixed to an accurately cut piece of wood, which fits the opening in the top of the vessel. The hollow in the base is filled with a piece of wood cut to match that hollow.

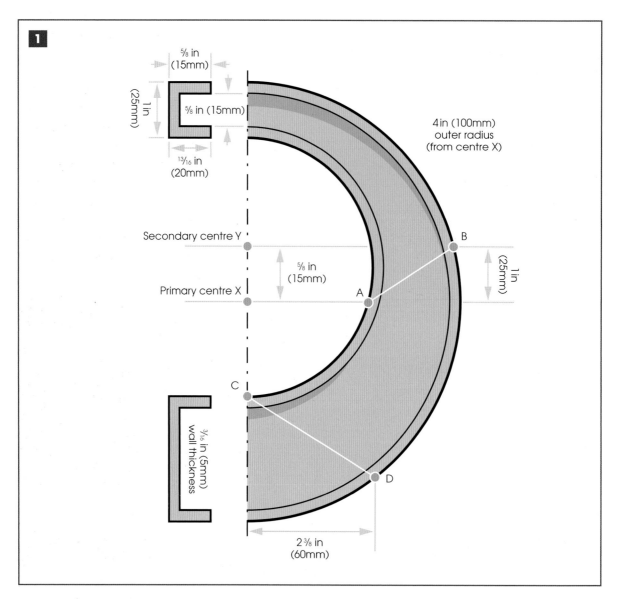

1

⅝ in (15mm)

1 in (25mm)

⅝ in (15mm)

¹³⁄₁₆ in (20mm)

4 in (100mm) outer radius (from centre X)

Secondary centre Y

⅝ in (15mm)

Primary centre X

A

B

1 in (25mm)

C

³⁄₁₆ in (5mm) wall thickness

D

2 ⅜ in (60mm)

Colouring the vessel

11 Prepare the vessel's surface by cleaning and sanding to it a fine finish. The surface will now be sprayed, so work in a well ventilated area and, if you have one, place the work in a spray booth. If you do not have a spray booth then a large cardboard box on its side will work well. Using automotive spray, apply a coat of filler primer. Allow to dry and then lightly clean using fine wire wool. Next, using matt white paint, spray the whole surface. Allow to dry.

On paper trace around the shape, back, front and two sides. On the traced outline draw out the chosen design. This will help decide where everything will fit. If you are going to hand paint the vessel using acrylic paints, it will not need to be masked as detailed below. Just mark out the design once the surface has been sprayed white and then begin painting. The black lines are applied when the painting is done, using a permanent black marker pen.

12 If you are going to airbrush the vessel, begin by carefully covering the vessel with masking tape and then draw the chosen pattern, in pencil, on the surface of the vessel. As opaque colours are to be airbrushed onto the surface here, the darkest colour will be spayed first. Select those areas and, using a scalpel, carefully cut around the chosen edges marked on the masking taped surface. Remove the masking tape from these areas (carefully setting the pieces of cut tape to one side) to expose the area to be coloured. As there will be a black line marked around these coloured areas, there will be a little leeway. Press the cut edges of the masking tape to make sure that paint is not sprayed under the edge by mistake.

13 Set the vessel in the spray booth. Switch the compressor on, fill the airbrush reservoir with paint and, pointing the airbrush to the side, away from the vessel, press the button on the airbrush to allow the flow of air. Now gently draw the button, still depressed, towards you until a spray of coloured paint is seen. Slowly draw the airbrush across the work. Apply a thin, even coat. Leave for a few minutes for the paint to dry and then apply a second, thin coating. Leave this to dry, continuing to add coats until the required density of colour is achieved. If the airbrush is blasting the paint off the surface, pull it away from the work and allow a lighter spray of paint to be applied. When all the chosen colour has been applied, pour the remaining paint from the reservoir into its paint pot. Fill the reservoir

with water and spray through until the airbrush is thoroughly cleaned. It may take several reservoirs of water to achieve this.

14 Leave until the paint is thoroughly dry before replacing the pieces of masking tape to cover the newly sprayed areas. Cut replacement pieces if they do not lie flat or fit cleanly. After two colours have been applied, remove all the masking tape and recover the vessel with new tape. Mark out the coloured sections again before cutting out the next areas to be painted. Once all the areas have been coloured **S** , use the black marker pen, the circle templates and the rule to mark the black line boundaries **T** .

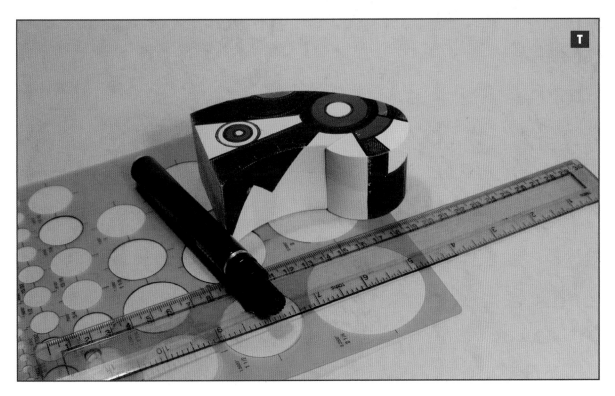

COCKEREL, IGUANA AND KIWI

The Cockerel vessel, with lid, in the foreground, is turned from oak. This wood was chosen because when the surface is wire brushed it shows an almost sculpted grain pattern. Add to that the ease with which it can be ebonized and the combination is irresistible. The Kiwi, the larger of the three, bends over almost out of balance pecking at the ground, while the Iguana, with its saw tooth punk headdress, stands quite upright.

Cockerel tools and materials

In addition to the tools and materials shown on page 17 you will need:

- A 9in- (230mm-) diameter by ⅞in- (22mm-) thick piece of planed oak
- A 5½in- (140mm-) long by 2⅜in- (60mm-) square piece of hardwood for the finial

Preparation

1 Mark a centre line through the oak blank, in line with the grain, on both sides of the blank. On one side mark the precise centre point clearly. This will be centre X, the primary centre. Measure ⅝in (15mm) from X along the centre line to locate centre Y. This will be the secondary centre. At each of these centres drill a ⅜in (9mm) hole at 90° to the face of the work. Fit this blank to the faceplate with the bolt through the primary centre X and tighten it down onto the faceplate.

2 Take a glass jar and place a piece of wire wool inside. Pour ordinary vinegar into the jar and set aside. On card, mark and cut out a template as shown in the diagram **1**.

Turning the vessel

3 Turn the edge of the blank clean and square to the face. From that edge, measure and mark in pencil, along the marked centre line towards the centre of the work, first ³⁄₁₆in (5mm), which will be line A, then 1⅜in (35mm), which will be line B, followed by 1⅝in (40mm), line C **A**. Between the two lines at ³⁄₁₆in (5mm) and 1⅜in (35mm) turn a hollow to match the template that you have cut out **B**. Sand that internal hollow but leave the edges sharp and clean.

4 Undo the centre nut and remove the partly worked blank from the coach bolt. Replace the blank with the bolt through the secondary centre Y and then retighten the nut so that the blank is firmly fixed to the faceplate. Rotate the work by hand. As the blank is held off-centre it will be seen

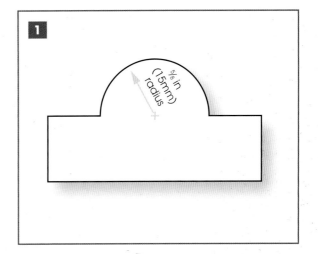

1

⅝ in (15mm) radius

A

B

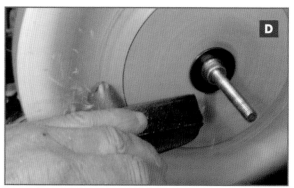

that when the centre line is horizontal the distance between the edge and centre Y will be about 5³⁄₁₆in (130mm) on one side and about 4in (100mm) on the other side. Arrange the blank so that the centre line is horizontal and the shorter distance to the centre is closest to the turner. Place a pencil on the originally marked line A. Rotate the work by hand and mark that pencil circle. Next, again with the blank arranged with the shorter distance closest to the turner, place the pencil on the originally marked line B. Rotate the work by hand and mark that pencil circle **C**. Switch the lathe on and turn a hollow, to match the template you have already cut, between the marked pencil circles **D** **E**. Very carefully sand the hollow leaving the edges sharp and clean. Remove the part turned piece from the lathe. The waste wood between the two turned hollows may now be chiselled out **F** **G**.

5 Remove the blank from the bolt, flip it over and replace it with the bolt in the primary centre X. Tighten the nut securely and make sure that the blank runs true. Measure in ¹³⁄₁₆in (20mm) from the edge and mark a pencil line. This is the top

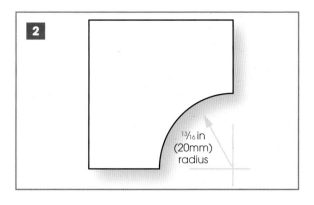

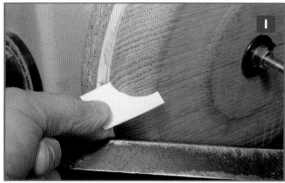

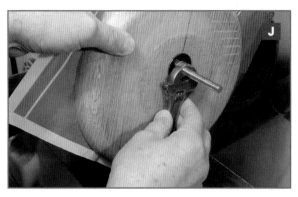

point of the curve, which may now be turned **H** using the card template based on the diagram above right **2**. Sand this outer curve smooth **I**.

6 Remove the blank from the bolt. The blank will now be fixed, hollow face down, on the secondary centre Y with a newspaper/glue joint to hold it firmly to the faceplate. Tighten the bolt to press the blank firmly onto the faceplate **J**. Leave overnight to dry.

Again, arrange the blank as previously described with the shorter (approximately 4in/100mm) distance from the edge to the centre closest to the turner. Mark, using a pencil, 1⅝in (40mm) in from that edge **K**.

7 Set the shelf tool rest in the tool post. Switch the lathe on and turn in, using a square-end tool, on the centre side of that marked pencil line. Make sure that the tool cuts at 90° to the face of the work. When the tool reaches the face plate, stop. The bolt can be undone and the centre section removed **L**. Turn the edge of this inner hollow **M** to match the template used in

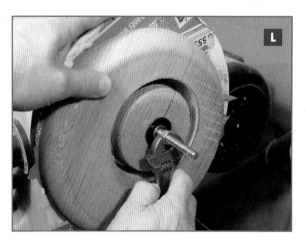

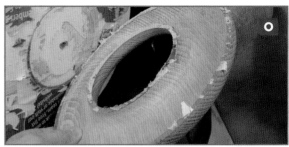

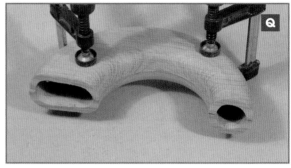

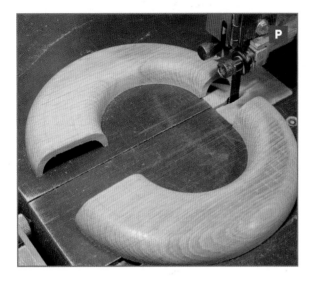

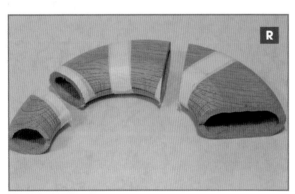

step 5 **N** . Sand the edge smooth. The piece may now be released from the newspaper/glue joint **O** by tapping wood wedges into the join line.

8 Take the turned blank to the bandsaw and cut through the marked centre line **P** . (Now the benefit of retaining that pencil line can be seen.) The two halves may now be carefully glued together **Q** . Using the diagram on the facing page **3** , mark out a card template by drawing from centre X to point P and locating the two points U and V. Using the template, mark the required shape onto the glued blank. This may now be cut on the bandsaw **R** . Sand the whole piece and then trace the opening in the base. Cut a piece to fill the base opening and glue in place. When the glue has dried, sand the base clean. Once the vessel has been vigorously scrubbed with a wire brush to expose the grain, giving it a sand blasted look, its surface needs to be blackened.

Ebonizing oak with vinegar and wire wool

9 First wipe the piece with water to raise the grain. Allow to dry and sand clean. Paint the surface of the oak with the vinegar/wire wool solution and very quickly the surface will blacken. In this photo of the partially blackened work **S** ,

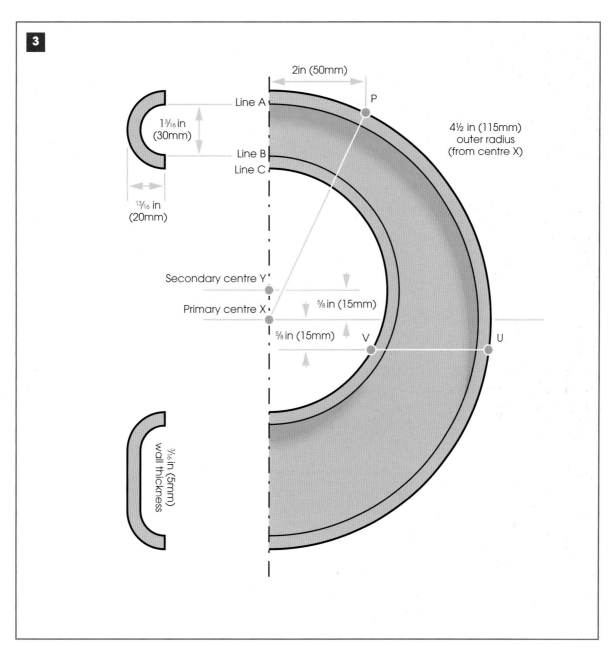

3

2in (50mm)

Line A

1³/₁₆ in (30mm)

Line B
Line C

¹³/₁₆ in (20mm)

P

4½ in (115mm) outer radius (from centre X)

Secondary centre Y

Primary centre X

⁵/₈ in (15mm)

⁵/₈ in (15mm)

V

U

³/₁₆ in (5mm) wall thickness

the difference between the treated wood and untreated can clearly be seen. A chosen polish is applied to the surface to complete it.

Turning the finial

10 The blank for the finial is held between centres and a spigot is turned so that it may be held in a chuck. The dimensions of the finial are shown in the diagram **4**. For full details of turning the finial see the 'Chinese' vessel project, page 49. Once the finial has been turned it is sprayed a buff colour to contrast with the ebonized finish.

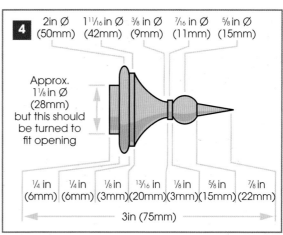

4

2in Ø (50mm)   1¹¹/₁₆ in Ø (42mm)   ³/₈ in Ø (9mm)   ⁷/₁₆ in Ø (11mm)   ⁵/₈ in Ø (15mm)

Approx. 1⅛ in Ø (28mm) but this should be turned to fit opening

¼ in (6mm)   ¼ in (6mm)   ⅛ in (3mm)   ¹³/₁₆ in (20mm)   ⅛ in (3mm)   ⅝ in (15mm)   ⅞ in (22mm)

3in (75mm)

IGUANA

Like the Cockerel, the Iguana is made from planed oak, but this time with a little twist; a bright yellow comb is fitted between the two halves of the vessel to create something quite unexpected.

Iguana tools and materials

In addition to the list at the beginning of the previous project (see page 63), which includes the size of the oak blank, for the Iguana you will need:

- ¼in (6mm) MDF
- Yellow spray paint

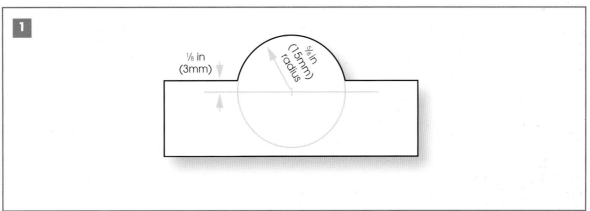

1

Preparation

The preparation for producing the Iguana style of vessel is exactly the same as the Cockerel, as it uses the same wood, at the same diameter and thickness (see page 63).

Turning the vessel

Follow the same procedure as described when turning the Cockerel vessel (see pages 63–68) but with the following important differences:

1 On the top surface, into which the hollow is turned, measure first ¼in (6mm) from the edge followed by 1⅜in (35mm). Turn a hollow into the area between these two lines using the template shown in the diagram above as a guide **1**. You will notice that the depth of the hollow is ⅛in (3mm) less than it was for the Cockerel. This is to allow the shaped spine (which is ¼in/6mm thick) to be fitted seamlessly between the two halves when they are joined.

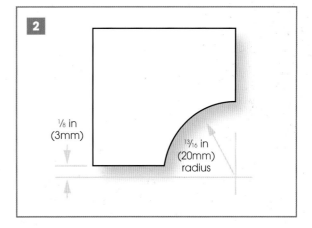

2

2 Continue to turn the top surface as before, offsetting the blank on centre Y and turning a second hollow, to match the same template. Use a mallet and chisel to clean the area left between the two turned hollows.

3 Flip the blank over and hold on the primary centre X. Now turn the blank down to ¹¹⁄₁₆in (17mm) thick. Turn the profile of the outer edge to match that shown on the template in the diagram above **2**. Sand the outer edge to

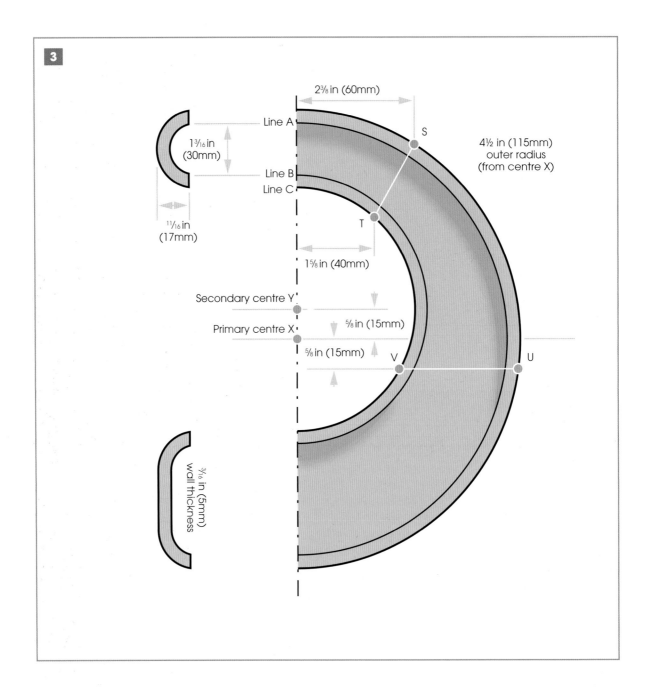

3

Line A

1³⁄₁₆ in (30mm)

Line B
Line C

2³⁄₈ in (60mm)

S

4½ in (115mm) outer radius (from centre X)

¹¹⁄₁₆ in (17mm)

T

1⁵⁄₈ in (40mm)

Secondary centre Y

Primary centre X

⁵⁄₈ in (15mm)

⁵⁄₈ in (15mm)

V

U

³⁄₁₆ in (5mm) wall thickness

a fine finish. Remove the blank and, using a chisel, flatten the hump around the two centre holes. Next, reposition the blank on secondary centre Y using a newspaper/glue joint to hold it firmly on the faceplate. Tighten the bolt down and leave until the glue dries.

4 On the shortest side of the centre line, with the shortest side closest to the turner, mark a pencil line 1⅞in (47mm) in from the edge. On the centre side of this line turn in at 90° to the surface, using a square-end tool, until the faceplate is reached. Remember to widen the groove so that the tool will not grip. This turned edge may now be rounded over to match the template used in step 3. Sand the edge clean and smooth. The piece may now be removed from the faceplate splitting the newspaper/glue joint.

5 Take the blank to the bandsaw and cut through the centre line to produce two mirror-image halves. Temporarily fit these together with masking tape. Refer to the diagram above **3** and cut a template from card as marked using lines UV and ST. Use the template to mark the shape on the temporarily held blank and then cut that shape **A**.

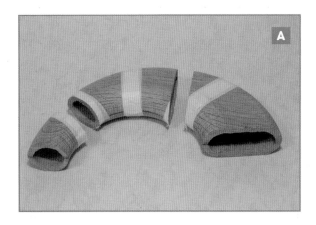

6 Now comes the fun part, the part that will open up a host of ways in which these vessels may be made to look so very different. Separate the taped halves of the vessel, and trace around one half on its inner and outer edges. Onto ¼in (6mm) MDF trace the thin curved inner and outer edges. On the outer edge extend the curve to produce a 'spine' **B** This may be any shape desired – in this case it is a saw tooth edge. Cut the shapes of the inner and outer edges from the MDF and clean them up thoroughly **C**. Spray paint the outer spine – here it has been sprayed a bright yellow – and ebonize the two halves of the vessel using the vinegar/wire wool solution. Surprisingly, the inner curved MDF filler piece also has enough tannin content for the vinegar/wire wool solution to work on it.

7 The parts are now carefully glued together, making sure that there is no glue squeeze out **D**. The ¼in (6mm) thickness of the spine and inner curved filler make up the ⅛in (3mm) turned away from each side, leaving the central hollow nicely round. Fit a thin piece of oak to fill the hollow in the base and then carefully polish the piece to finish. Creating a 'spine' to fit between the two halves opens up so many possibilities. The inner edges may be shaped, and the spine can be produced from many materials and in many colours.

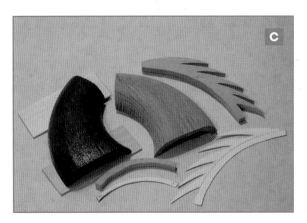

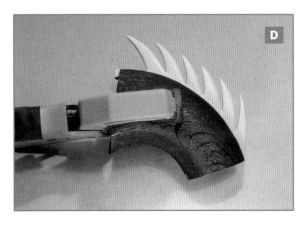

KIWI

The Kiwi vessel is made from $^{13}/_{16}$in- (20mm-) thick planed oak.
The finished surface has been burnt, scrubbed and ebonized to create
an interesting texture. Its sweeping, stretching form seems to be fighting
to keep its balance.

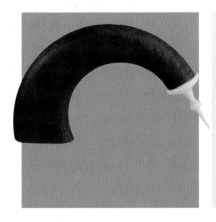

Kiwi tools and materials

In addition to the list of tools shown on page 17 you will need:

- A piece of planed oak 8¾in (220mm) in diameter by ¹³⁄₁₆in (20mm) thick
- Some fire bricks to create a hearth
- A propane torch
- Heat-resistant gloves
- Eye protection
- A piece of hardwood 5³⁄₁₆in (130mm) long by 2³⁄₁₆in (55mm) square for the finial
- Two small pill magnets

Preparation

Prepare the blank to the same sizes as for both the Cockerel and the Iguana (see page 63).

Turning the vessel

1 Turn the piece in exactly the same way as described in turning the Cockerel vessel (see pages 63–66). Once the blank has been cut into two mirror-image halves it may be glued together **A** .

2 The base of the piece is cut along line EF, as seen at the lower part of the diagram on page 75 **1** . As the centre of gravity will be well outside the base of the vessel it will always tip over, particularly when the finial lid is in place, so counter weights need to be glued into the bottom of the vessel before the base is fitted. This photograph **B** of a previous vessel shows how a counter weight can be glued in place. Now trace the opening at the base of the vessel and cut a thin piece of oak to match. Glue that piece in place.

Creating the surface texture

3 The surface of the vessel is to be burnt and wire brushed to expose the grain and create an interesting textured surface. Set the fire bricks, outdoors, to create a hearth. Using a propane torch, char the surface of the vessel **C** but do not overheat the work for the glued joint might open. Char the surface lightly, not too deep. All that is required is to soften the summer growth.

4 Once the work piece has cooled, scrub the surface with a wire brush **D** . This will brush away the softened summer growth and expose the hard

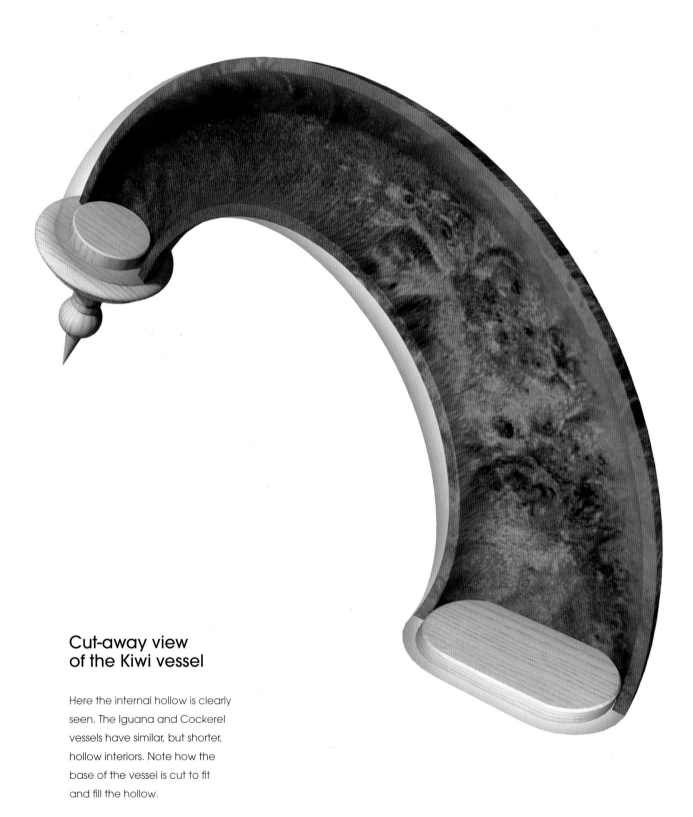

Cut-away view
of the Kiwi vessel

Here the internal hollow is clearly
seen. The Iguana and Cockerel
vessels have similar, but shorter,
hollow interiors. Note how the
base of the vessel is cut to fit
and fill the hollow.

winter growth rings. This process really exposes the grain pattern of the wood and, as it has been burnt, the surface is ebonized at the same time. To enhance this darkening, paint the surface with a vinegar/wire wool solution. The surface should be sealed using a matt finish.

Making the finial

5 The finial is turned in exactly the same way as shown in step 10 of the Cockerel vessel project (see page 67) **E** . Use small pill magnets, one set inside the vessel opening and the other into the edge of the finial **F** so that they attract one another, to hold it in place.

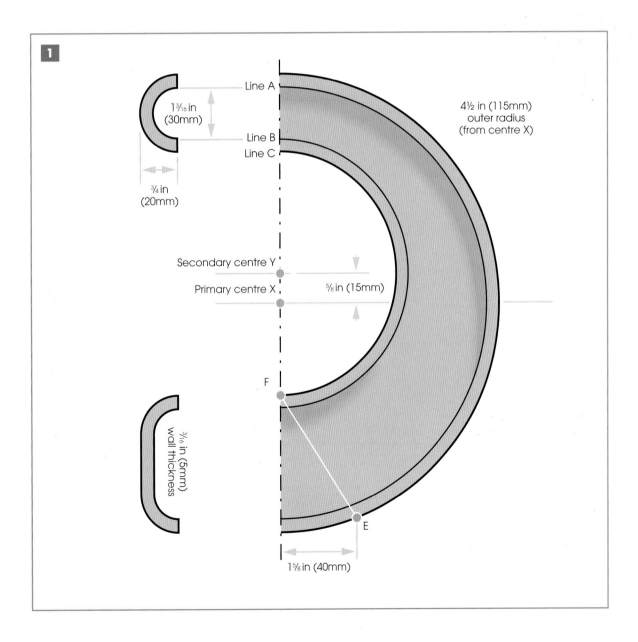

1

Line A

1³⁄₁₆ in (30mm)

Line B
Line C

³⁄₄ in (20mm)

4½ in (115mm) outer radius (from centre X)

Secondary centre Y

Primary centre X

⅝ in (15mm)

F

³⁄₁₆ in (5mm) wall thickness

E

1⅝ in (40mm)

SNAKE

Curved rectangular hollow sections cut from two different rotational axes produce this unexpected, twisted hollow form. The concept of the same profile from different axes may cause you to see turned work in a different light.

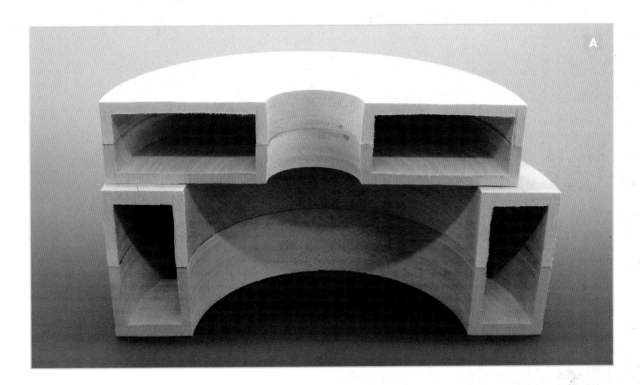

Two matching forms

This particular shape is an interesting development of the hollow forms already described. Here a hollow rectangular section is produced but it is turned, first with the longer side of the rectangular hollow in line with the rotation of the lathe to produce the first form and second with the longer side of the rectangular hollow at 90° to the rotation of the lathe to produce the second form. The two forms have the same cross section, but at right angles to each other  A . At first, the idea of alignment of a side to the lathe rotation may seem difficult to grasp but, hopefully, as the working method is described all will become clear. Having these two forms with the same cross-section but aligned differently B will allow them, when cut into segments, to be rejoined to produce a contorted hollow form. Having understood the turning method used to produce these parts, it will be seen that the idea may be further developed using different alignments, for example at 45° to the lathe rotation, using different cross-sections or even adding other forms to the end of the piece  C . Of course, the size of the cut segments may also be varied to contort the finished form even further. It is very exciting coming upon an idea with so much to explore.

Tools and materials for the first form

In addition to the list of tools and materials shown on page 17 you will need:

- A piece of hardwood, 8¾in (220mm) in diameter by 1⅜in (35mm) thick, planed both sides (sycamore is used here)
- A roll of 2in- (50mm-) wide masking tape

Preparation for the first form

1 Draw a pencil centre line, in line with the grain, on the front and back of the prepared sycamore blank. Mark the centre point X. At that point drill a ⅜in (9mm) hole at 90° to the face to fit the bolt of the captive nut faceplate.

2 Apply PVA glue to the captive nut faceplate and the underside of the blank. Press a sheet of newspaper onto the glued surface of the faceplate and then fit the blank down onto that. Fit the bolt through the drilled hole and onto the captive nut in the faceplate. Lock the blank tightly against the faceplate and leave until the glue dries. When the glue has dried, turn the edge flat and perfectly square to the face of the work. Alternatively fit the blank in place with the bolt holding it tightly down. Turn the outer edge of the blank flat and perfectly square to the face of the work and then, using a hot melt glue gun, apply a weld of glue around the edge of the blank as it joins the faceplate. Here a hot melt weld is being applied to a much larger blank **D**.

Turning the first form

3 The blank is now ready to turn. Begin by setting the shelf tool rest into the tool post. Measure and mark the following: ³⁄₁₆in (5mm) in from the edge towards the centre to mark line A; 1⅜in (35mm) in from the edge to mark line B; and 1⅝in (40mm) in from the edge to mark line C **E**. The diagram below shows the profile we are aiming to achieve **1**.

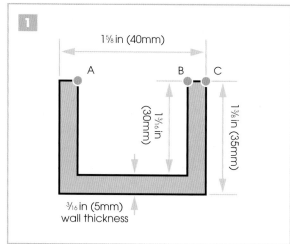

4 On the square-end tool, ,using typist's correction fluid, mark a point 1³⁄₁₆in (30mm) from the cutting edge 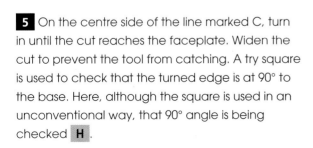 **F** . Between lines A and B, using the square-end tool supported on the shelf tool rest, turn down to the 1³⁄₁₆in (30mm) depth mark. Alternatively, a long and strong tool supported on an ordinary tool rest may be used to turn the hollow and to carry out the following step **G** . Whichever method is used, make sure that the edges of the hollow are cut square to the face of the work and the base of the hollow is perfectly flat.

5 On the centre side of the line marked C, turn in until the cut reaches the faceplate. Widen the cut to prevent the tool from catching. A try square is used to check that the turned edge is at 90° to the base. Here, although the square is used in an unconventional way, that 90° angle is being checked **H** .

6 Clean up the whole piece. If a newspaper/glue joint has been used, tap fine wood wedges into the joint line to release the blank from the faceplate **I** . If a hot melt weld secures the blank to the faceplate then press a disc of wood against the blank using the revolving centre to apply that pressure. The weld may then be safely turned away **J** , and the blank removed **K** .

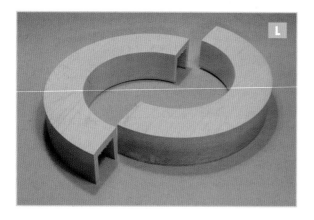

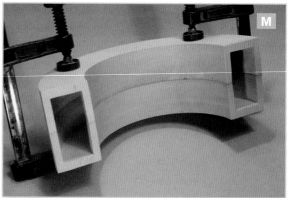

7 Take the blank to the bandsaw and cut the piece, along the marked centre line, into two mirrored halves The two halves may be glued together, using yellow glue, to produce the first of the hollow forms .

Tools and materials for the second form

In addition to the same tools and equipment as needed for the first form (see page 78), you will need:

- An 8¾in- (220mm-) diameter by ¹³⁄₁₆in- (20mm-) thick piece of hardwood planed both sides (sycamore is used here)

Preparation for the second form

8 Mark, in pencil, a centre line on both sides of the blank across the diameter and in line with the grain. At the centre of the blank drill, at 90° to the surface, a hole that is the same diameter as the bolt used for the captive nut faceplate. Fit the blank onto the captive nut faceplate either using the newspaper/glue method or with a hot melt weld. In either case use the bolt to fix the blank firmly in place.

Turning the second form

9 Turn the edge of the blank square to the face of the work. Mark point D ³⁄₁₆in (5mm) in from that edge towards the centre. The diagram below **2** shows the profile we are aiming to achieve in this case. From the same edge, measure 2⁹⁄₁₆in (65mm) in towards the centre to locate point E. Again from the edge, towards the centre, measure 2¹³⁄₁₆in (70mm) to locate point F.

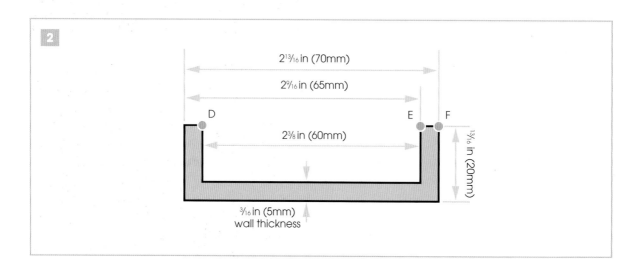

2

2¹³⁄₁₆in (70mm)

2⁹⁄₁₆in (65mm)

D   E   F

2⅜in (60mm)

¹³⁄₁₆in (20mm)

³⁄₁₆in (5mm)
wall thickness

10 The central bolt may now be removed (unless a hot melt weld is used to hold the blank, in which case it must remain until completion). Switch on the lathe and hold the pencil, in turn, at points D, E and F to mark pencil circles. If the first form is now held against the marked pencil circles they should match **N**.

11 Fit the shelf tool rest into the tool post and take the square-end tool. Measure from the cutting edge along the shank ⅝in (15mm) and mark that position using typist's correction fluid. Using the square-end tool, turn the area between lines D and E ⅝in (15mm) deep. Make sure that the base is flat, true and clean and that the edges are cut square to the face **O**.

12 Using the square-end tool, turn into the blank on the centre side of line F. Make sure that this cut is square to the face. Widen the cut as work progresses to prevent the tool from gripping **P**.

13 Sand the whole piece to a good finish but do not round over edges. Using fine wood wedges and a hammer, remove the part-turned work from the wood faceplate **Q**.

14 Clean off the newspaper/glue using a scraper. Take the piece to the bandsaw and cut through the centre line to produce mirror-image halves. These may be glued together using yellow glue **R**.

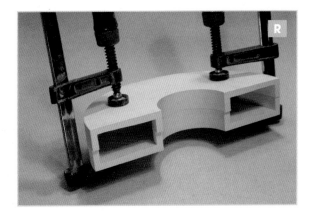

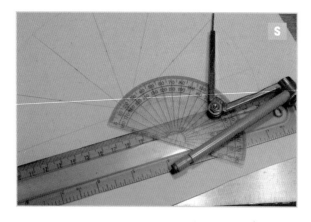

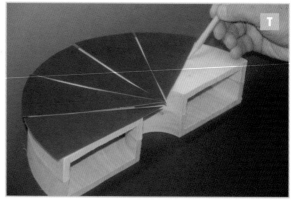

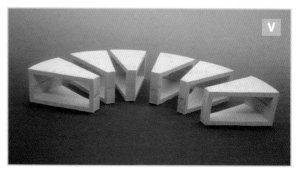

Marking out the segments

15 Take a piece of card and draw a 4⅜in-(110mm-) radius semi-circle. Using a protractor mark six 30° wedges 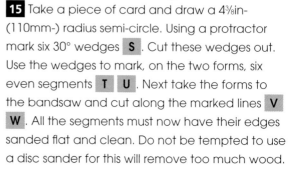 S . Cut these wedges out. Use the wedges to mark, on the two forms, six even segments **T** **U** . Next take the forms to the bandsaw and cut along the marked lines **V** **W** . All the segments must now have their edges sanded flat and clean. Do not be tempted to use a disc sander for this will remove too much wood.

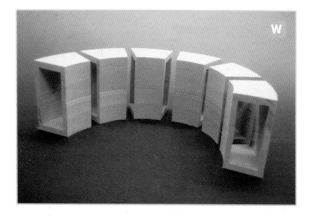

Assembling the parts

16 There is no real order in which to assemble the parts **X** . Here the parts were fixed alternately. Just try the pieces together, hold them temporarily in place with tape and, when satisfied, the joining may start. Use a good waterproof yellow glue. This will hold end grain to end grain joints firmly. Cut two 4¾in (120mm) lengths of masking tape and place on one side. Take the first and second chosen pieces. Apply glue, sparingly, to the edges to be joined. (Squeezed out glue will have to be cleaned off later.) Press the joint together. Take the piece of masking tape and wrap it around the joined area. Adjust the two pieces until the joint is

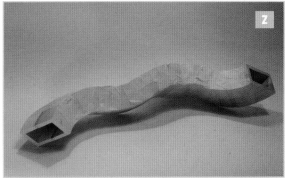

as even as possible. (Sometimes the joints are not perfect fits. Do not be concerned; make the joint fit as closely as possible. Any unevenness can be smoothed out later.) Take the second piece of tape and wrap that around the joint. Check the joint line again, adjusting if necessary, before moving on to glue the next segment **Y** **Z** . When the glue has set the tape may be removed. The joint lines may be cleaned using a small drum sander on a flexidrive **A1** .

Decorating the vessel

17 This first form of decoration **B1** requires a sprayed base coat of white paint. The form is covered with masking tape and a series of rectangular areas are uncovered. These are then sprayed red with a grey shading added to their edges. These coloured rectangles are then masked and further rectangular areas are opened and sprayed blue. The blue areas also have a grey shading spray to their edges to give a shadowed depth. Finally, the white between the coloured rectangles is textured with a series of cut marks that show the brown wood beneath.

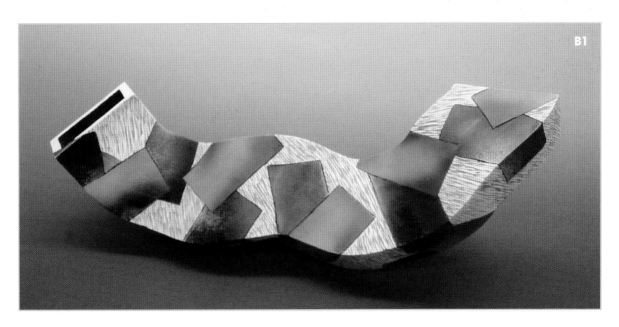

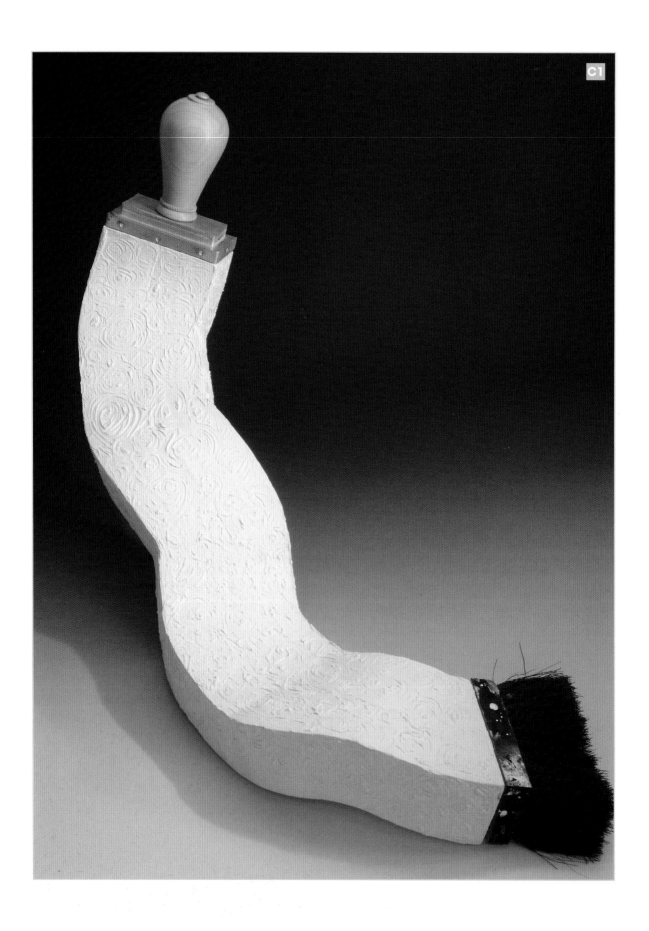

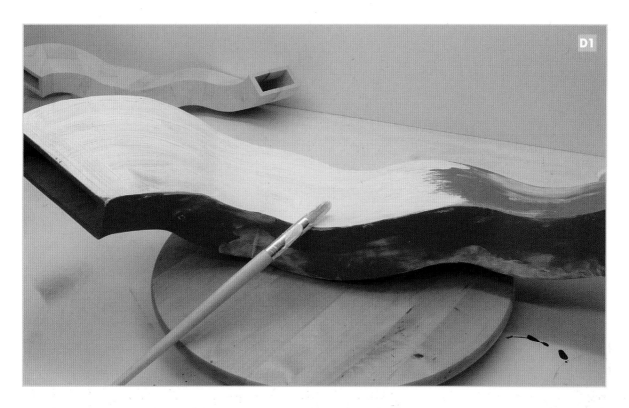

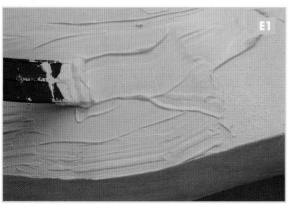

18 A more interesting and amusing decoration of the snake is this huge brush, approximately 2ft (600mm) long **C1**. This larger snake form has been given a 'texture paste' base coat to even out the surface **D1**. This base coat is allowed to dry before a heavier coat of texture paste is applied **E1**. A small dowel is used to create swirling patterns in the paste to simulate the decorators' nightmare – Artex **F1** **G1**. Finally the whole piece is sprayed white and a handle is fixed at one end and a brush at the other.

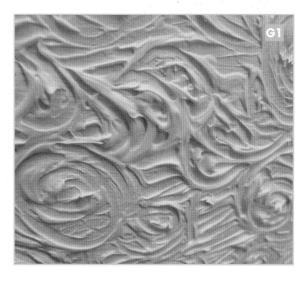

ZEBRANO

The choice of zebrano for this piece is quite deliberate. The strong linear grain clearly shows the joined parts but, equally, binds the whole vessel to become a complete piece.

Tools and materials

In addition to the list of tools and materials shown on page 17 you will need:

- A piece of ⁷⁄₈in- (22mm-) thick by 8¾in- (220mm-) diameter zebrano (or similar)

Wood with character

Having cut and reassembled basic turned hollow forms to produce the Snake project (see page 76) it seemed appropriate to look at the off-centre forms to discover how it would look if they were treated in a similar manner. In this case the piece is turned from a piece of zebrano, which has a very defined grain pattern. This grain pattern will exaggerate the movement created by the joined parts. Any similar strikingly patterned wood will work. Alternatively, use a wood with little or no grain or spray the piece white. This will show off the shape and allow its surface to be decorated.

Preparation

1 On the 8¾in- (220mm-) diameter disc of zebrano mark a centre line, on both sides, in line with the grain. Mark the centre point – this will be the primary centre X. Measure from X along the centre line ⅝in (15mm) and mark that position.

This will be the secondary centre Y. At the two marked points drill a hole with a ³⁄₈in (9mm) diameter at 90° to the face of the work. This matches the bolt used to fit the captive nut on the faceplate.

Turning the vessel

2 Fit the prepared disc of wood to the faceplate with the bolt through primary centre X. Turn the edge clean and at 90° to the face of the work. From the *edge* measure and mark the following lines: ¼in (6mm) for line A, followed by 1½in (38mm) for line B and 1¾in (44mm) for line C. The distance between A and B should be 1¼in (32mm). The diagram below **1** shows how these measurements relate to the profile we are aiming for.

3 On the square-end tool, using typist's correction fluid, mark a point ²¹⁄₃₂in (16mm) away from the cutting edge. Fit the shelf tool rest into the tool post, set the square-end tool on the rest and turn between lines A and B down to ²¹⁄₃₂in (16mm) deep **A**. The depth mark on the square-end tool will act

1¾ in (44mm)

1½ in (38mm)

A   B   C

1¼ in (32mm)

⁷⁄₈ in (22mm)

²¹⁄₃₂ in (16mm)

¼ in (6mm) wall thickness

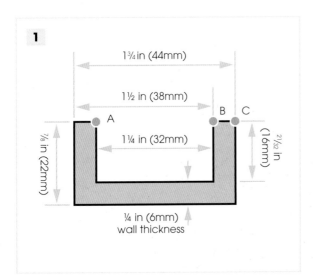

as a guide. Make sure that the base of the hollow is flat and the edges are square to the face. Clean up the hollow but do not round over any edges.

4 Remove the piece from the faceplate and relocate, still turned side up, on the secondary centre Y. Fit the bolt in place and lock down tight. Rotate the work by hand and bring the marked centre line horizontal. Make sure that the shortest part of that centre line is closest to the turner. Place a pencil so that it touches line B (the cut edge of the hollow) on that centre line. Rotate the lathe by hand to mark that pencil circle **B**. This will produce a pencil circle that is off-set from the original cut but just skims it.

5 Using the square-end tool set on the shelf tool rest turn a 1¼in (32mm) wide hollow on the inside of this marked line. It too will be ²¹⁄₃₂in (16mm) deep **C**. Using a mallet and wood chisel clean away, and level, the crescent of waste wood between the two channels to leave an eccentric hollow **D**. If the centre line has been cleaned off mark it again **E**.

6 Remove the piece from the lathe and flip it over. The piece will now be held on the nut/bolt faceplate on the secondary centre Y with a newspaper/glue joint **F**. Leave until the glue has thoroughly dried before turning this piece. Rotate the work by hand and bring the marked centre line horizontal. Make sure that the shortest part of that centre line is closest to the turner. It is important that it is the shortest part. From

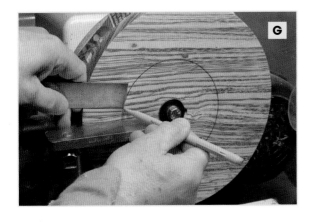

the edge mark 1¾in (44mm) in along the centre line. Using a pencil held on that point, mark a circle 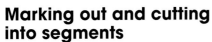 G .

7 On the centre side of that line turn in using the square-end tool at 90° to the face. Widen the cut so that the tool does not grip. Stop when the tool reaches the faceplate H . Remove the bolt and the inner core so that the turned face can be cleaned. Again, avoid rounding edges. The piece may be removed from the faceplate. Using fine wood wedges and a hammer I , take the work to the bandsaw and cut along the marked centre line to produce two mirror-image halves. These may be glued together to produce a hollow form J .

Marking out and cutting into segments

8 Take a piece of card and, using a pair of compasses, mark a 4¾in (120mm) radius semi-circle. Upon that semi-circle, using a protractor, mark six segments each with a 30° angle. Cut the segments out. Arrange the segments on the turned blank and mark out those six segments K .

Take the marked blank to the bandsaw and cut it into six equal pieces **L** .

9 Hand sand the cut edges of the segments, making sure that they are perfectly flat. The segments may now be glued together. As the cross-section of the piece is regularly shaped and as the cuts have been made radially, the cut faces of adjoining parts will match and fit well even when one of the segments is rotated through 180°. Arrange the segments on the bench to see how they fit **M** . Taking the largest and second segment first, test the fit. They are to be arranged so that the internal curve of one sits against the external curve of the next.

10 Using a good, waterproof, yellow glue, spread the glue upon both edges to be joined. Bind the joint tight with masking tape, making sure that the joint is perfectly aligned before moving to the next joint. Repeat with the next three segments. Having tested the segments together, we found that when all six were aligned to produce the new form it just did not look right. By leaving off the last segment the vessel looked far more balanced so, in this case, only five segments were glued together **N** .

11 When the glue has dried, fit the base as described in step 12 of the 'Chinese' vessel (see page 46), using a matching piece of zebrano. Clean the base flat when its glued joint has dried. The edges can now be smoothed into one another using a small drum sander **O** . The flat faces are sanded with a palm sander and when complete the vessel may be polished.

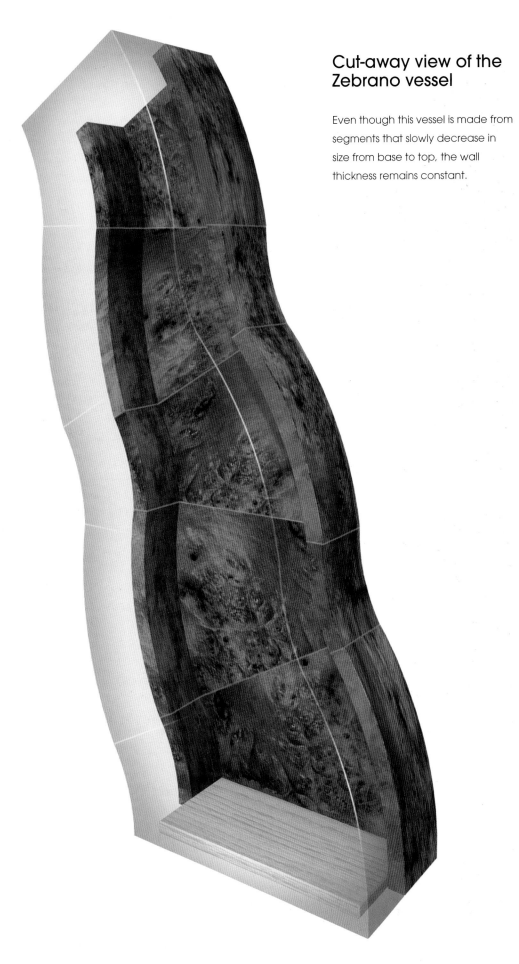

Cut-away view of the Zebrano vessel

Even though this vessel is made from segments that slowly decrease in size from base to top, the wall thickness remains constant.

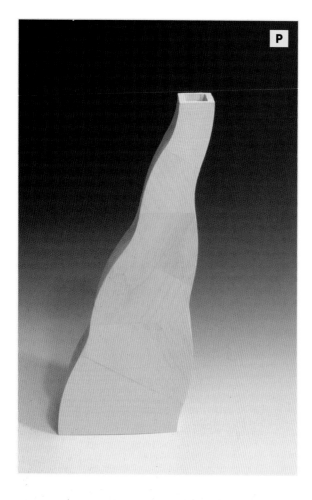

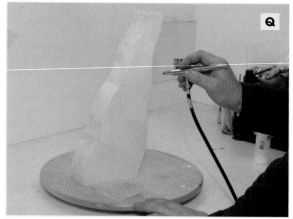

'Tear and spray' decoration

Here we see the base form upon which this 'tear and spray' design was applied. This dramatic piece P was turned, cut and reassembled exactly as described above. It was made from a 17½in- (440mm-) diameter by 1⅝in- (40mm-) thick piece of sycamore. The distance between the primary (X) centre and the secondary (Y) centre was 2in (50mm). The channel cut was 1in (25mm) wide, the wall and base thickness was ¼in (6mm) and the finished piece stands 15in (380mm) high, all made from a blank that would normally be turned into a bowl.

Preparing the surface

To achieve this decorative look, you will need a roll of low-tack masking tape, white gesso filler and white and black acrylic paints, either for an airbrush or in spray cans. The vessel may be left as natural wood or have a white base coat. If it is to have a natural wood undersurface then skip step 12. Any end grain surfaces must be very cleanly cut.

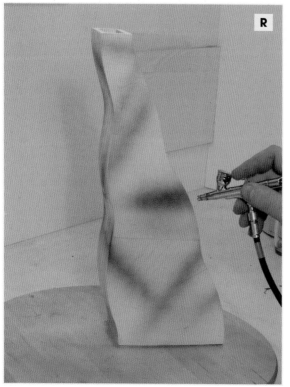

12 Fill any tearout in the grain using a white gesso paste. When it is dry, sand back to a fine finish. The vessel itself should also be sanded so that it has a fine surface. Spray the vessel with an even coat of white acrylic Q. Spray random colour (or black as shown here R) to break up the surface. If the colour is too strong, overspray it with white.

13 Tear random strips of masking tape so that both long edges are torn and the ends are irregular points. Apply the torn strips to the vessel sympathetically, so that they generally follow the same direction and flow around the vessel S . Consider the tear shapes as impressions of claw marks T . Make sure that the masking tape is firmly pressed onto the surface of the vessel.

14 Spray the whole vessel black U . When spraying, direct the jet of paint so that it is square on to the work. Keep the direction of the spray at 90° to the taped surface. An angled spray can force the edge of the masking tape up, allowing the black paint to go underneath. Several light coats will prevent runs in the paint. Leave the paint to dry and then carefully peel off the torn masking tape strips V . Here we see the completed Zebra striped vessel W , but there's no reason why it has to be black and white.

ELEPHANT VESSEL

From the one basic process used in this project a wide variety of
vessels may be made. Take a look at the silhouettes at the end of this
chapter to see just how many there can be.

Tools and materials

In addition to the list of tools and materials shown on page 17 you will need:

- A piece of hardwood, 8in (200mm) in diameter by ¹³⁄₁₆in (20mm) thick, which has been planed both sides (here maple was used)

Using unequal segments

Having cut the previous blank into six equal segments it seemed like an interesting idea to alter the segment size (cutting a 1/6 segment, a 2/6 segment and a 3/6 segment), fit those parts together and check the result. The vessel produced from unequal segments looked far more like a ceramic form than a turned form and the variations are many (see the silhouettes on page 103). The vessels produced in this way have a rectangular hollow interior that tapers from a small opening at the top to a wider hollow at the base mimicking the shape of an elephant.

Preparation

1 Take the planed, circular wood blank and mark a matching pencil centre line, with the grain, on both sides. Mark the primary centre as X. From point X measure along the pencil centre line 1in (25mm) and mark that point as Y, the secondary centre. At points X and Y accurately drill a ⅜in (9mm) hole at 90° to the surface.

Turning the vessel

2 Now fit the blank onto the captive nut/bolt faceplate with the bolt through the primary centre marked X. Tighten it down onto the faceplate. Using the ⅜in (9mm) gouge turn the edge flat, clean and at 90° to the top surface. From the edge mark ³⁄₁₆in (5mm) along the centre line to locate point A. Again, from the edge mark ¹³⁄₁₆in (20mm) along the centre line to locate point B. The diagram below left **1** shows how the measurements relate to the profile we are creating.

3 Set the shelf tool rest into the tool post. On the square-end tool mark a point, using typist's correction fluid, ⅝in (15mm) from the cutting edge. Using the marked square-end tool, cutting at centre height and set upon the shelf tool rest, turn down between points A and B to ⅝in (15mm) deep **A**. Make sure that the base of the hollow is flat and true and the edges are cut square to the top face. Clean up the cut hollow but do not round over any sharp edges. Loosen the bolt and remove the work from the faceplate.

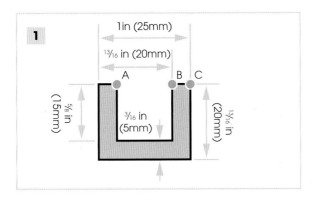

1in (25mm)

¹³⁄₁₆ in (20mm)

A   B C

⅝ in (15mm)

³⁄₁₆ in (5mm)

¹³⁄₁₆ in (20mm)

A

4 Fit the bolt through the secondary centre Y. Spread PVA glue on the surface of the faceplate and the underside of the blank. Place a piece of newspaper onto the glued surface of the faceplate and then press the blank onto that newspaper. Now fit the bolt through into the captive nut and tighten down, ensuring that the blank is held tight against the faceplate. Leave until the glue has fully dried. (The hot melt glue weld could be used as an alternative method of fixing.)

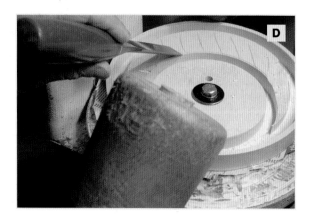

5 When the glue has fully dried, bring the shelf tool rest close to the work. Rotate the lathe by hand to make sure that nothing catches and bring the marked centre line so that it is horizontal. Make sure that the shortest part of that line is closest to the turner. It is important that it is the shortest part of the line. Place the pencil point on the position originally marked as A, ³⁄₁₆in (5mm) in. Rotate the lathe by hand and draw that pencil line around the blank. Again set the blank so that the centre line is horizontal and the shortest part of that line is closest to the turner. Place the pencil on the position originally marked B, ¹³⁄₁₆in (20mm) in. Rotate the lathe by hand and draw that pencil line around the blank. Now there will be two lines set ⅝in (15mm) apart **B**.

6 Using the square-end tool, turn down to the marked depth, ⅝in (15mm), between lines A and B. The edges must be turned square to the face of the work and the base turned flat. The crescent-shaped waste wood can now be chiselled away, leaving a flat, crescent-shaped base **C** **D**.

7 Measure ³⁄₁₆in (5mm) from line B, towards the centre, and mark that line (line C) **E**. On the centre side of line C, turn in square to the face until the tool reaches the faceplate. Remember to widen the cut to prevent the tool from being gripped **F**.

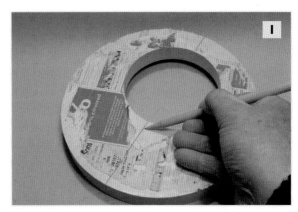

8 Now loosen the bolt and remove the centre core . This will allow the internal cut edge to be sanded clean. Do not round over any edges. The blank may now be removed from the faceplate using wood wedges and a hammer . Turn the blank over and make sure that the centre line is still visible . Take the blank to the bandsaw and cut along that centre line.

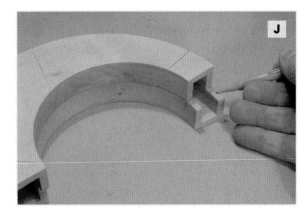

9 The two halves may now be glued together. The newspaper glued to the wood surface may be removed before or after the halves have been joined. Occasionally, the halves do not fit precisely . This is not a problem, for the end of the vessel can be trimmed neatly to finish.

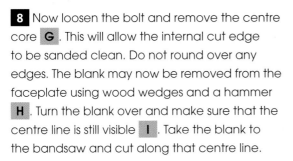

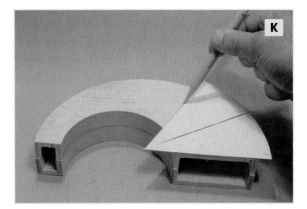

10 On card draw an 8in- (200mm-) diameter half circle. Using a protractor, mark six equal 30° divisions. Here the divisions are arranged, from the thick end of the vessel, 2/6 followed by 3/6 and the final 1/6. Mark those divisions in pencil . Take the glued vessel to the bandsaw and cut along the marked lines to give three sections.

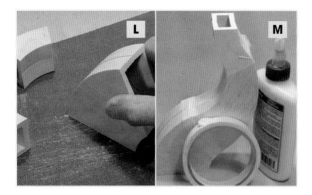

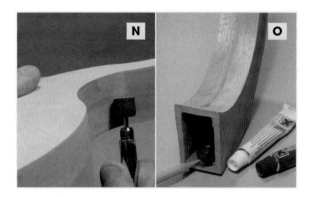

Hand sand the cut edges L . Test the edges to be joined and only when they are a perfect fit can they be glued together.

11 Glue the three parts together, reversing the middle section to create the snaking form, using a yellow glue and binding the joint with masking tape M . When the glue has dried the edges can be sanded smooth N .

12 If another arrangement of segments, for example 2/6, 3/6, 1/6, has been used the vessel can be out of balance. If this is the case a counter weight needs to be glued inside the base of the hollow O . If the counter weight is, first, temporarily held in place with tape its effectiveness can be checked. The base may now be fitted to the vessel (see the 'Chinese' vessel, step 12, page 46). Clean up the whole vessel, and it is now ready for any style of surface decoration that will enhance the form.

Bronzing decoration

Here we see a bronzed burr wood form with added real bronze 'drips' that are left after casting P .

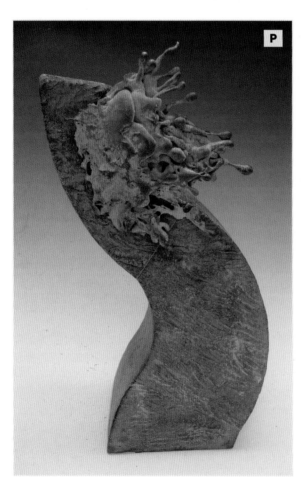

To carry out the bronzing using Nick Agar's recipe you will need:
- A gas torch and firebrick hearth
- A fire extinguisher
- Facemask and heat-resistant gloves
- A spray bottle of water
- A soft wire brush, preferably with brass bristles, or on old scrubbing brush
- Black and/or brown acrylic paint or spray
- Copper or bronze acrylic paint
- Vinyl gloves
- Blue and yellow acrylic pigments
- Soft wax
- Cleaning cloth
- Copper-coloured Goldfinger paste
- Wax, oil or lacquer to finish

Cut-away section of the Elephant vessel

The wide, hollow base tapers up to the small top opening while the wall thickness remains even.

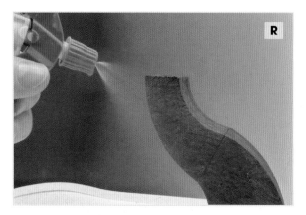

Preparation

To achieve the best results choose a good hard (the harder the better) piece of burr wood from which to make the chosen piece. Here an Australian gum burr has been used. The natural swirling grain, holes and hollows in this form of wood will accentuate the applied bronzing effect. If you do not have burr wood then the surface of your chosen wood can be cut, gouged and textured to provide the indented surface. In this case the wood surface will not need to be burnt in preparation for the bronzing. To really bring out the pattern in the burr grain the wood surface has to be scorched. This will soften some parts of the wood and allow them to be scrubbed away to leave a more irregular surface. As the piece is made up from several glued sections it is essential to choose a glue which is heat resistant. We have found that Titebond 2 resists moderate heat.

For safety when burning the wood surface, the following precautions need to be followed:
• Work outside in an area clear of any combustible materials
• Make sure that the area is relatively draught free
• Wear a protective mask and heat proof gloves
• Have a fire extinguisher ready
• Ideally work within a firebrick hearth

The technique

13 Char small areas of the wood until a red glow is seen **Q** . Use the spray bottle of water to damp the glowing area, stopping the piece from continuing to burn **R** . Avoid overheating the glue joints. Here we can see the deeply charred surface of the wood **S** .

14 When the piece has been charred all over, take a soft, preferably brass bristle, wire brush and vigorously clean the surface of any loose charred carbon **T** . A Scotchbrite pad will help remove the final stubborn patches.

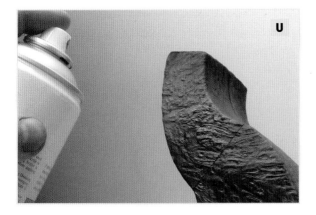

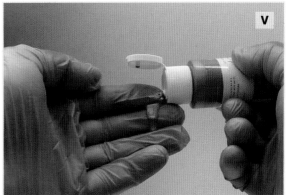

15 Use black or brown acrylic paint to cover the surface and leave to dry. A paint brush can be used but no brush marks must remain. A spray is better U . The paint seals the surface and provides a 'key' for the next layer of water-based paint.

16 Use a bronze or copper acrylic paint to cover the surface. This is best applied using two fingers (wearing vinyl gloves) sparingly in a random fashion V W . For a more authentic look use two or three different colours of bronze or copper. If too much paint has been applied don't panic, allow it to dry and lightly paint over with black or brown acrylic to tone it down. X shows the vessel at this stage. This is just a base coat to give the necessary depth before the verdigris wax is applied.

17 Prepare the verdigris wax. In a bowl mix blue and yellow powder pigments Y . To the now green pigment add clear soft paste wax and mix well Z .

A1

B1

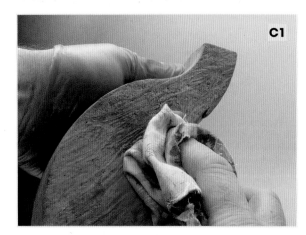

C1

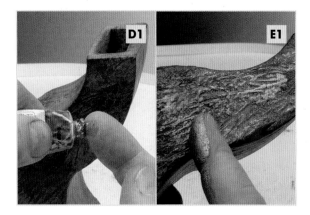

D1

E1

18 Rub the verdigris wax over the surface of the wood using vinyl gloved fingers **A1** to achieve this finish **B1**.

19 Using a lint-free cloth, rub away the excess wax from the high points to fine tune the bronze effect **C1**, but don't be too hasty. Let the wax dry a little as you want some to remain on the surface. You may need a toothbrush to remove the heavy deposits. This is important as the wax is not a filler. It will shrink in the pockets where it has been left too thick.

20 Next use a tube of copper Goldfinger to highlight the grain pattern **D1**. Squeeze a small amount (about the size of a grape pip) onto your index finger. Rub thumb and finger together to give a thin even coat. Make sure that there is no excess wax around the edge of your finger.

21 Very gently glide your finger over the surface to highlight the high spots of the textured surface **E1**. When applying this copper-coloured wax try to imagine how a real bronze piece will look **F1**. Leave to dry and then apply wax, oil or lacquer finish. Here we see the finished vessel with a bronzed spinning top disc applied **G1**.

F1

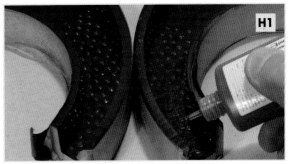

their insides sprayed black **H1**. 3D paint is being applied as dots (check the Internet for 3D paint). When the paint has dried, the two halves may be joined and cleaned up, the base can be fitted and then the exterior may be worked upon. This is an interesting effect, for when the piece is complete it seems impossible that decoration has been added to the deep interior.

Assembly variations

Choices have to be made when marking out and cutting the segments of the part finished piece. Looking at the silhouettes below **2** you can see that these variations on the segment assembly produce quite different finished vessels. Some are more interesting than others. Here all the segments are based upon a 30° angle, or multiples of 30°. Experiments have not yet been tried with other angular cuts.

Adding decoration to the inside

22 There is always the possibility of adding decoration to the inside of the form but this must be done before the two halves have been joined. Here we see the two halves once they have had

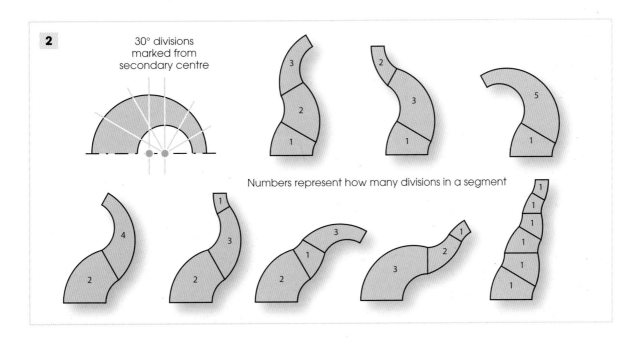

30° divisions marked from secondary centre

Numbers represent how many divisions in a segment

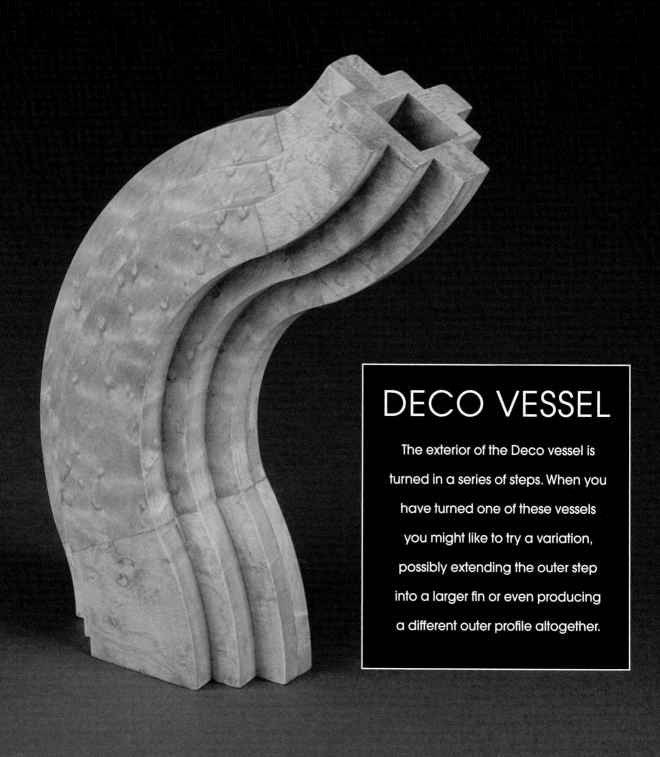

DECO VESSEL

The exterior of the Deco vessel is
turned in a series of steps. When you
have turned one of these vessels
you might like to try a variation,
possibly extending the outer step
into a larger fin or even producing
a different outer profile altogether.

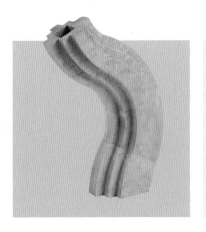

Tools and materials

In addition to the list of tools and materials shown on page 17 you will need:

- A 9in- (226mm-) diameter by 1in- (25mm-) thick piece of hardwood planed both sides. Here Bird's-eye maple is used

A turned exterior

The vessels produced to this point have had quite plain exteriors, leaving large areas for decoration. So why not turn the outside and allow that to be the main feature of the piece? By turning a series of steps both on the inner and outer edges of the blank, turning on the two centres as before, cutting into segments and reassembling, another interesting vessel has been developed. Of course, there are many other developments to be made along similar lines, as long as the shape turned on the inner edge is the same as that turned on the outer.

Preparation

For those working in inches it is advisable to make a drawing first to ensure that the dimensions will work effectively. The imperial dimensions have been translated from metric and that translation *may* not be precise.

1 Take the cut, circular blank and mark a pencil line through the marked centre and in line with the grain of the wood on both sides and in alignment. Mark the centre as X. From that marked primary centre measure ⅝in (15mm) along the pencil centre line and mark that secondary centre as Y. At points X and Y drill a ⅜in (9mm) hole at 90° to the face of the work. Fit the work to the captive nut/bolt faceplate using the ⅜in (9mm) bolt set through the primary centre X. Make sure that the work is firmly fixed to the faceplate.

Turning the vessel

2 Turn the edge of the blank flat, true and at 90° to the face of the work. From that turned edge measure and mark, along the pencil centre line,

first ¾in (18mm) to locate line A. From line A measure, along the pencil centre line towards the centre, ⁹⁄₁₆in (14mm) to locate line B **A**.

3 Fit a shelf tool rest into the tool post. On the square-end tool measure ½in (12mm) from the tip and mark using typist's correction fluid. Set the square-end tool on the shelf tool rest so that it will cut at centre height **B**. Turn down to ½in (12mm) deep between lines A and B, making sure that the base of the cut is good

and flat **C** . Now remove the blank from the faceplate and relocate it with the bolt through the secondary centre Y.

4 Rotate the lathe by hand, bringing the marked centre line horizontal and with the shortest distance closest to the turner. Measure from the edge at that point, along the centre line, towards the centre again ¾in (18mm) and ½in (12mm) and mark these lines. This time these lines will just skim the cut hollow at one point and be off-set for the majority of the marking. With the square-end tool set at centre height, turn between these new marked line to a depth of ½in (12mm) **D** .

5 Using a mallet and wood chisel clean off the crescent of waste wood between the two turned hollows. When satisfied that the, now crescent-shaped hollow is flat bottomed, the piece may be removed from the captive nut faceplate. Flip the blank over so that the cut hollow faces the faceplate and fit the bolt through the primary centre X, making sure that it is firmly in place. Check also that the blank runs on centre, adjusting the position if necessary. Now rotate the lathe by hand until the marked centre line is horizontal. From the edge measure along the centre line, towards the centre, first ¹³⁄₃₂in (10mm) to locate line C then a further ¹³⁄₃₂in (10mm) to locate line D, followed by a further ¹³⁄₃₂in (10mm) to locate line E **E** .

6 Using the square-end tool set on the shelf tool rest, turn down between line C and the outer edge to a depth of ¹³⁄₁₆in (20mm). This will leave a ³⁄₁₆in- (5mm-) thick rim. Again using the square-end tool set on the shelf tool rest, turn down from line D, towards the outer edge, to a depth of ¹³⁄₃₂in (10mm). This will leave two turned steps on the outer edge **F** . Clean up and polish the outer profile without rounding over the edges.

7 Remove the blank from the faceplate. Apply a coat of PVA glue to the surface of the faceplate and to the underside rim (with the crescent-shaped hollow) of the blank. Fit the bolt through the secondary centre Y, press a piece of newspaper (large enough to cover the base of

Cut-away view of the Deco vessel

The stepped outer shape tapers
from a wide base to a narrow top.

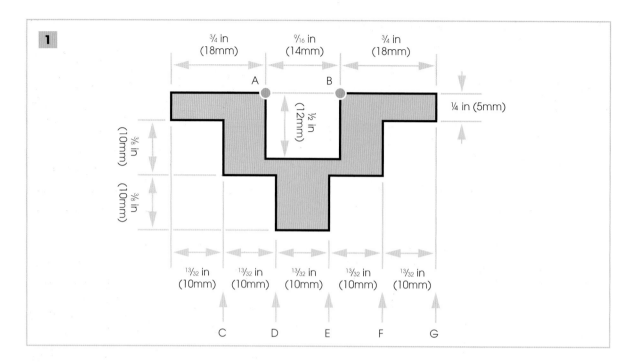

1

¾ in
(18mm)

⁹⁄₁₆ in
(14mm)

¾ in
(18mm)

A   B

½ in
(12mm)

¼ in (5mm)

³⁄₈ in
(10mm)

³⁄₈ in
(10mm)

¹³⁄₃₂ in
(10mm)

¹³⁄₃₂ in
(10mm)

¹³⁄₃₂ in
(10mm)

¹³⁄₃₂ in
(10mm)

¹³⁄₃₂ in
(10mm)

C   D   E   F   G

the blank) onto the glued surface of the blank and press it against the faceplate, fitting the bolt so that it tightens on to the captive nut. Tighten down so that the blank is held firmly upon the faceplate. Leave until the PVA glue has thoroughly set. When the glue has set, rotate the lathe by hand so that the centre line is horizontal and the shortest side of that line is closest to the turner. From line D measure ¹³⁄₃₂in (10mm) towards the centre to locate line E **1**. From line E measure a further ¹³⁄₃₂in (10mm) to locate line F, and from line F measure ¹³⁄₃₂in (10mm) to locate line G. Mark those lines upon the blank **G**.

8 On the inside of line G turn in at 90° to the surface using a square-end tool set upon the shelf tool rest with the tool set at centre height. Widen the cut towards the centre to prevent the tool from being gripped in the cut **H**. When the cut reaches the faceplate, halt. Remove the bolt from the drilled hole and remove the central core with a firm tap. This should break the newspaper/glue joint **I**.

9 Again using the square-end tool on the shelf tool rest, turn a ¹³⁄₁₆in- (20mm-) deep step between lines F and G **J**. Between lines F and E turn a ¹³⁄₃₂in (10mm) step **K**. Sand and polish the cut

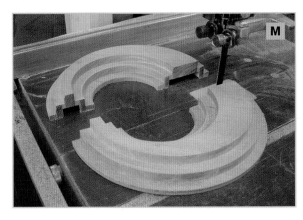

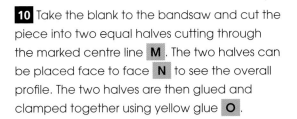

steps without rounding over the edges. Now, the newspaper/glue joint may be split using thin wood wedges to release the turned blank from the faceplate **L** .

10 Take the blank to the bandsaw and cut the piece into two equal halves cutting through the marked centre line **M** . The two halves can be placed face to face **N** to see the overall profile. The two halves are then glued and clamped together using yellow glue **O** .

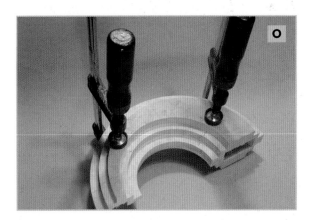

11 On card, mark six 30° segments and cut into sections of two segments, three segments and one segment. Mark on the blank, from the wide base, first the two-segment section and then the three-segment section, which leaves one segment at the top. Cut these lines accurately. The segments may now be glued together, remembering to rotate each segment through 180° before fixing. Use yellow glue on these end grain joints and bind those joints tightly with masking tape while the glue sets. Finally sand the whole piece and re-polish **P** .

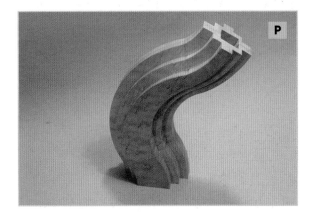

WHISPER

This vessel was turned from a 1³⁄₁₆in- (30mm-) thick piece of planed kopie.
A bland wood was chosen to allow the sinuous, snaking form to be
clearly seen. A small amount of decoration is added to provide a 'lift'.

Tools and materials

In addition to the list of tools and materials shown on page 17 you will need:

- A plain hardwood disc 7³⁄₁₆in (180mm) in diameter by 1³⁄₁₆in (30mm) thick
- Two slicing tools (made to the dimensions shown in the diagram below **1**)
- Three templates cut from card (see diagram, page 113)

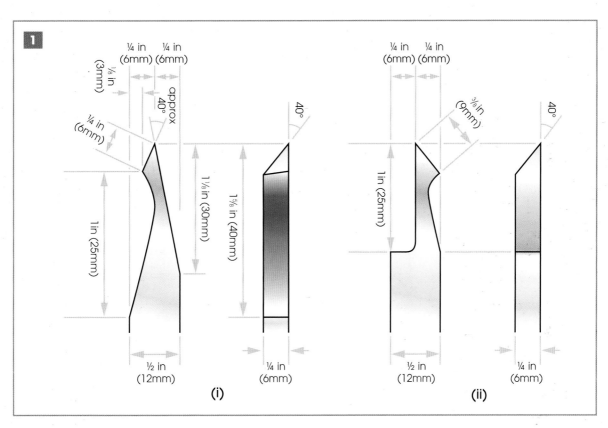

1

¼ in (6mm) ¼ in (6mm)
⅛ in (3mm)
approx 40°
¼ in (6mm)
40°
1⅛ in (30mm)
1⅝ in (40mm)
1 in (25mm)
½ in (12mm)
¼ in (6mm)
(i)

¼ in (6mm) ¼ in (6mm)
⅜ in (9mm)
40°
1 in (25mm)
½ in (12mm)
¼ in (6mm)
(ii)

Disappearing sides

The shape that developed when a square hollow, this time set on the diagonal, was turned off-centre was to some degree quite unexpected. The base of the vessel has six sides twisting and tapering to just four sides, with two faces disappearing like a whisper of smoke. This piece was turned from kopie, which is usually used as a substrate in furniture making. Kopie is such a stable, plain-grained wood that it lends itself to decoration.

Preparation

1 Take the 7³⁄₁₆in- (180mm-) diameter by 1³⁄₁₆in- (30mm-) thick disc of hardwood and mark a pencil line across the diameter, in line with the grain, on both sides of the blank. Mark the centre of the blank X (primary centre). Measure from the primary centre X ⅜in (9mm) along the centre line to locate the secondary centre Y. At centres X and Y drill, at 90° to the surface, a ⅜in (9mm) hole (to fit the faceplate bolt). Fit the disc to the captive nut faceplate with the bolt through the primary centre X. Tighten the bolt to fix the blank firmly onto the faceplate.

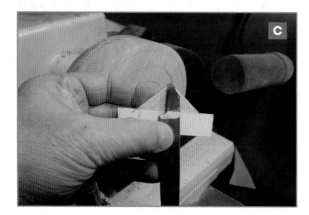

2 Turn the outer edge flat, true and at 90° to the face of the work. From the *edge* measure along the centre line first ³/₁₆in (5mm) to locate line A. Again from the *edge* measure along the centre line 1³/₃₂in (27.5mm) to locate line B. From the *edge* measure along the centre line 2³/₁₆in (55mm) to locate line C. Double check the measurements before proceeding **A**.

3 Following the dimensions in the diagram on the facing page **2**, draw onto card and cut out these three templates. Now take slicing tool (i) **3** and set it on template 2 with the tip in line with the point and the angled edge in line with the angled side. Using typist's correction fluid, mark a line on the tool in line with the base line on the template **B**. Now take slicing tool (ii) and set it on template 1 with the tip in line with the point and the angled edge in line with the angled side. Using typist's correction fluid mark the base line on the tool in line with the base line on the template **C**.

4 Take slicing tool (i) and set it upon the shelf tool rest so that it is cutting at centre height. Set the tool so that the marked base line is parallel to the face of the work. This places the cutting edge in the correct position to give a good, starting guide. Bring the point of the slicing tool in line with line B. Touch the point of the tool on that line to produce a light cut. This provides a 'stop'. Now move the tool a small distance to the left and slice towards the 'stop' **D**. Continue the slicing cuts and occasionally work down line

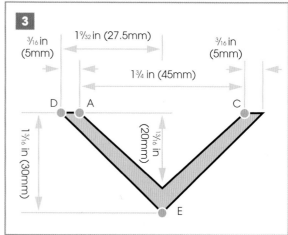

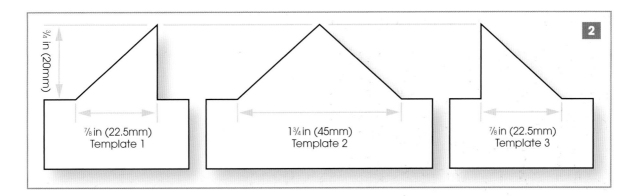

¾ in (20mm)

⅞ in (22.5mm)
Template 1

1¾ in (45mm)
Template 2

⅞ in (22.5mm)
Template 3

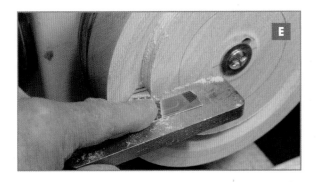

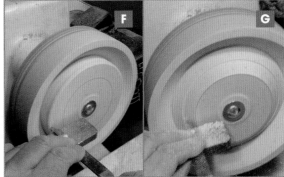

B deepening the 'stop' but making sure that it the cut at the 'stop' is at 90° to the surface of the work 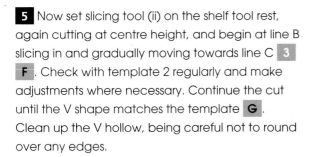 E . Test the cut regularly using template 1 and adjust where necessary. When the cut reaches line A and it matches the template, halt.

5 Now set slicing tool (ii) on the shelf tool rest, again cutting at centre height, and begin at line B slicing in and gradually moving towards line C **3** F . Check with template 2 regularly and make adjustments where necessary. Continue the cut until the V shape matches the template G . Clean up the V hollow, being careful not to round over any edges.

6 Remove the blank from the faceplate and relocate the bolt in the secondary centre Y. Tighten the bolt so that the blank is firmly fixed to the faceplate. Rotate the work by hand so that the pencil centre line is horizontal and the shortest side of that line is closest to the turner. Place the pencil so that it touches the edge of line C, rotate the lathe by hand to draw a pencil circle – the circle • in the diagram on the right **4** . This circle will just touch the original sloping cut on line C but will be off-set from it H .

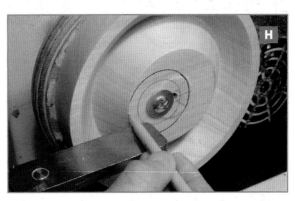

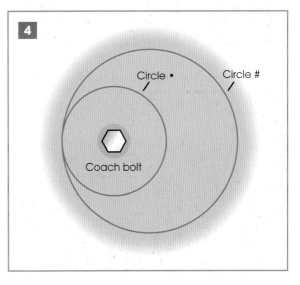

4

Circle •
Circle #
Coach bolt

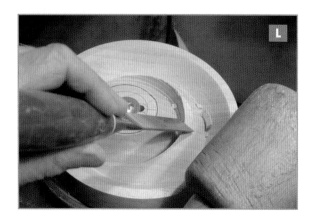

7 Rotate the lathe by hand to bring the centre line horizontal and so that the shortest side of that line is closest to the turner. Measure from line C (where the pencil circle, just marked, touches the edge of the sloping cut) ⅞in (22.5mm) towards the left along the centre line (i.e. into the V we have just cut), and mark another pencil circle (circle # in the diagram on page 113) **I** .

8 Set tool (ii) on the shelf tool rest so that it cuts at centre height. Hold the tool, with base line mark parallel to the face of the work, so that the tip is on circle •. Switch the lathe on and lightly push the tip of the tool into circle • to produce a 'Stop'. Slice towards that 'Stop' slowly increasing the slope and, checking by using template 3, adjust the cut where necessary **J** . Here we see the completed cut with the waste crescent of wood remaining between the two sloping faces **K** . This waste crescent can now be chiselled flat **L** . Remove the blank from the lathe and if there is any raised wood around the area of the bolt hole it can now also be chiselled flat.

9 Mount the piece on the captive nut faceplate with the turned V pressed against the faceplate. The bolt is passed through the primary centre X and the blank is bolted down firmly, making sure that it runs on centre. Adjust where necessary. Rotate the lathe by hand, bringing the marked centre line horizontal. Measure from the edge towards the centre 1³⁄₃₂in (27.5mm) and mark a pencil circle at that point. This circle describes edge E, and the edge of the blank where it touches the faceplate is edge D **M** .

10 Using a gouge, set on a conventional tool rest, join edge E to edge D with a clean, straight, sloping cut. To help judge if the cut is progressing evenly and at the correct angle look at the distance from the start point E and the start of the cut . Compare this with the distance between the finish point D and the finish of the cut in progress **O**. If those distances are the same then the sloping face will be at the correct angle. If they are different then make adjustments in the cut until they are the same. When satisfied with the sloping face, sand carefully, avoiding rounding over the edges. Remove the blank from the faceplate **P**.

11 Push the bolt through the secondary centre Y. Apply PVA glue to the faceplate and the underside edge of the blank. Press a sheet of newspaper onto the glued surface of the faceplate, locate the bolt in the faceplate hole and tighten the blank onto the newspaper/ glue faceplate **Q**. Leave until the glue is completely dry.

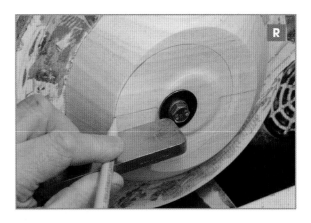

12 Rotate the lathe by hand until the centre line is horizontal and the *shortest* side is closest to the turner. Place a pencil where circle E touches the centre line and draw another pencil circle. This will be off-set from, but touch at one point, the original edge of circle E **R**. Rotate the lathe by hand until the centre line is horizontal and the *shortest* side is closest to the turner. From the point where the new, off-set circle touches the centre line measure, towards the centre, 1³⁄₃₂in (27.5mm). Mark that pencil circle as G **S**.

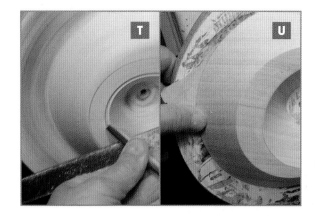

13 Using a square-end tool, set on the shelf tool rest to cut at centre height, turn in on the centre side of circle G. Next, widen the cut towards the centre to prevent the tool from being drawn into the work. Turn in until the faceplate is reached. The bolt may be removed and the centre plug broken away from its newspaper/glue fixing. The newspaper/glue joint will hold the blank allowing the inner sloping cut the be made. Change the shelf tool rest for a conventional tool rest. Using a gouge, join edge E to the base of the cut G with a clean, straight, sloping cut **T** . Carefully sand the sloping cut avoiding rounding over any sharp edges **U** .

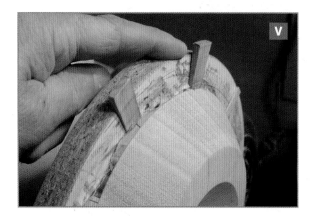

14 Use fine wood wedges, tapped in with a hammer, to release the blank from the newspaper/glue joint **V** . Using abrasive paper set on a flat surface the edges of the blank are cleaned removing the residual newspaper. Take the blank to the bandsaw and cut through the marked centre line **W** .

15 The two halves are now glued together using a yellow glue to create a curved hollow that has an hexagonal hollow at one end tapering to a square hollow at the other.

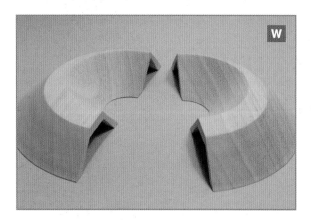

On a piece of card mark and cut a 7³⁄₁₆in- (180mm-) diameter semi-circle. Divide this semi-circle, using a protractor, into six segments, each with an included angle of 30°. Cut this marked semi-circle into three pieces as follows: one segment; three segments as a whole piece; and two segments as a whole piece. Lay the segments on the blank, starting at the wide end – one segment, the three-segment piece and the two-segment piece **X** . Mark out the edges of the segments on the blank. It's not easy holding and marking those segments, so take your time.

16 Take the blank to the bandsaw and cut through the marked lines, starting at the small end. Sand the cut ends by hand. Test the pieces, one piece rotated against the next, and when you are happy that the fit is good, glue the parts together using yellow glue, making adjustments where

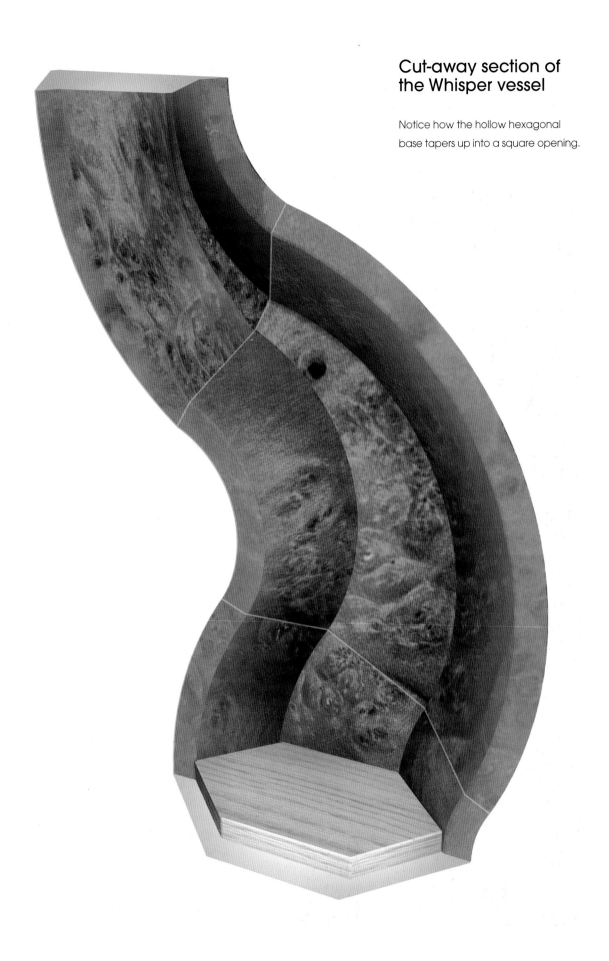

Cut-away section of the Whisper vessel

Notice how the hollow hexagonal base tapers up into a square opening.

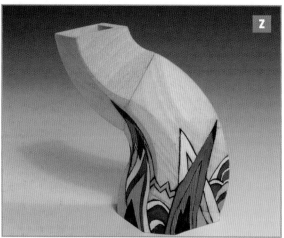

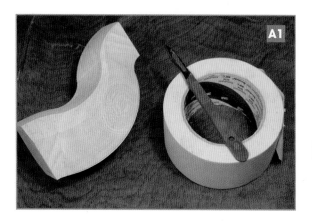

necessary. Use masking tape to hold the joints firmly together while the glue dries  Y . When the glue has dried, clean the form, sanding the joints so that they run easily into one another. To fit the base to the hollow vessel cut a ¼in- (6mm-) thick piece of the same wood as that used for the vessel. Trace the hexagonal hollow in the base. Transfer the shape to the ¼in- (6mm-) thick wood and cut to shape. Glue the base into the hexagonal hollow. When the glue has dried, sand off the base.

Decorating the vessel

A Clarice Cliff 'Bizarre' design was the basis for the decoration on this piece Z . It is easier to use the design only as an inspiration, for if the pattern is slavishly copied it will lose its impact. If you need ideas then look on the Internet and there you will find a large range of Clarice Cliff's work and designs, which are so inspirational.

17 As it is so difficult to remove pencil marks made directly upon the wood surface, start by covering the entire vessel with low-tack masking tape A1 B1 . Do not leave the tape on the work

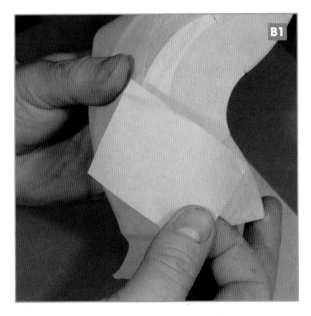

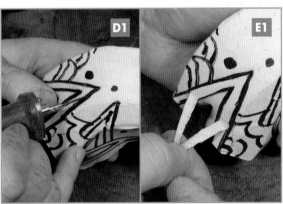

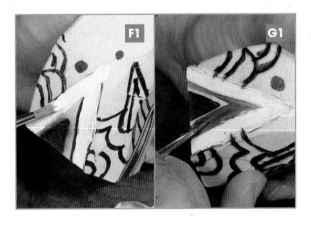

for any longer than necessary. Even though it is 'low tack' it will stick firmly if left too long. Using a black marker pen, draw the design directly upon the taped surface **C1**. The fact that the tape can be removed and the drawing reworked should give you more confidence in the drawing.

18 Warm up the poker pen. This will be used to burn down the marked lines. As you work, refine the lines of the pattern **D1**. The poker pen burns through the masking tape and burns lines upon the wood surface. These burnt lines frame the design. Once all the lines have been burnt use a brass bristle suede brush to carefully clear away any carbon from the pyrographed lines. Carefully peel back areas of tape to expose the parts to be painted, each colour in turn **E1**.

19 Using acrylic paint, paint between the lines with care **F1**. More than one coat of paint will be needed to produce the dense colour required. When the first colour has been applied to all those areas marked to receive them, move onto the next colour **G1** **H1**. Use the poker pen to re-mark the lines between the colours. Try to avoid paint leaching into the burnt grooves. If spirit stain is used to colour the vessel then the burnt lines will stop the colour from jumping across to the next patch.

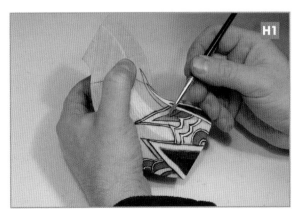

OUTSIDE
THE BOX

The two faces of this vessel are ideal

surfaces to display decorative

treatments. Then, having worked on

the outside of the box, why not think

'inside the box'?

Tools and materials

In addition to the list of tools and materials shown on page 17 you will need:

- Texturing tools
- A ⅜in (9mm) negative rake square-end tool
- ⅜in (9mm) and ¼in (6mm) bowl gouges
- Spirit stains and diffuser
- Liming wax and cloth
- Vinyl gloves

- 2 pieces of maple (or similar light-coloured wood) 9½in (240mm) in diameter by 1⅜in (35mm) thick with planed surfaces
- A piece of wood, for the jam chuck, 11³⁄₁₆in (280mm) in diameter by 1⅜in (35mm) thick. A wood-jawed chuck is an alternative to the jam chuck

Empty box

By joining two hollow forms (basic wide cylinders that have precisely the same diameter) edge to edge, an empty box is created. By cutting a wedge into that empty box, a vessel is created, as the illustrations show **1** **2**. By decorating the outside faces of that vessel, a piece of artwork is created.

Preparation

1 To turn the blanks, hold each of the matching maple discs in turn with the revolving centre on the precise centre of the wood and press it firmly against a faceplate held on the headstock of the lathe. The outer edge of each disc may then be turned so that it is flat and square to the face of the work. Both discs must be turned to exactly the same diameter. An exact dimension is not required but it is important that they are the same. By holding them in this manner, one face of each disc will have a central mark (from the revolving centre) and the other will be clear.

The jam chuck

2 Screw the 11³⁄₁₆in- (280mm-) diameter by 1⅜in- (35mm-) thick piece of wood centrally onto a metal faceplate. Turn its face flat and the edge flat and square to that face. Next, measure the

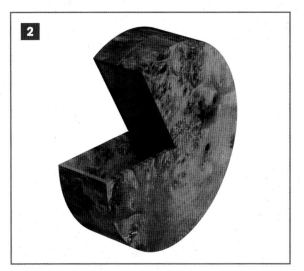

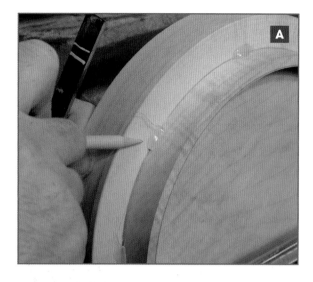

diameter of the two blanks and transfer that measurement to the face of the jam chuck. Using the negative rake scraper, turn a shallow, flat-bottomed hollow on the inside of the marked line. Test both blanks into the hollow. When the fit is tight turn the hollow so that it is flat bottomed and ¼in (6mm) deep.

Turning the vessel

3 As the blank will be hollowed and the base needs to be about ¼in (6mm) thick, first check the thickness and make a note of it. It will be too late when it is held in the jam chuck and cannot be measured. Press the blank into the jam chuck, making sure that it runs true. If you are at all unsure that the jam chuck will hold the work sufficiently firmly, run a few hot melt glue 'stitches' around the edge **A**. (It is important not to allow hot melt glue to run into any gap between the blank and the jam chuck. Do not allow the gun to heat the glue so that it is too runny. It is best when it has the texture of thick toothpaste.) Turn the face flat, and sand through the grades of abrasives down to 400 grit. Make sure that there are no scratch marks, for these will pick up the colour and the wax that are applied later.

Using the texturing tools

The two larger texturing tools shown above **B** were initially developed for spiral decoration on spindles. As with many tools, Nick Agar has, over time, developed their use on flat and curved surfaces, as you will see here.

When decorating the surface, there are several important points to remember:
• Always check that the texturing wheels run freely before starting.
• Use the texturing tools with the lathe speed at approximately 1,000 rpm.
• Set the tool rest twice the diameter of the texture wheel away from the face of the work.

• When using these tools, have the bevel of the tool facing the wood.
• When starting to texture the wood surface, make light contact and then slowly increase the pressure. The pattern will vary with the pressure and the density of the wood used.
• The angle at which the texturing tool approaches the work will affect the pattern that is produced.
• It is a good idea to practise with these texturing tools to gain an understanding of how they work and the patterns they produce before starting on an important piece of work.

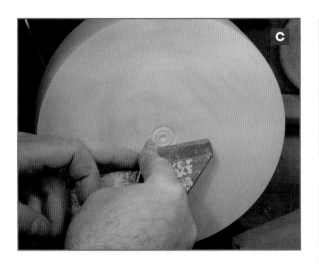

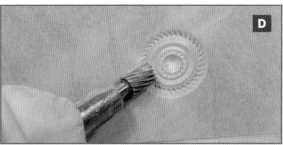

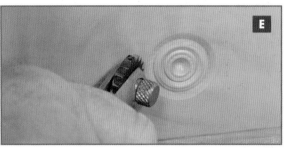

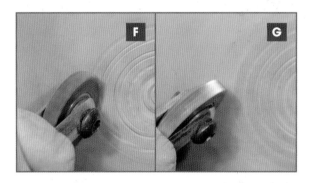

Decorating the surface

4 Start by using the ¼in (6mm) gouge to turn a small hollow at the centre surrounded by two or three rings **C**.

Now the texturing tools can be applied to the surface of the wood. It really is a case of practising with the tools to understand what surface textures can be produced. Here we see the barrel-shaped tool being applied to the edge of one of the turned hollows **D**.

The smaller texturing wheel produces a 'Catherine wheel' star-burst effect **E**. This was slightly hampered by the texture wheel jamming briefly (it can happen to anybody: I should have read the first point above), but to no ill effect. If, by chance, the decoration is unsatisfactory it can be turned away, the area sanded fine again, and the work started again.

Applying the wheel at different angles will produce different effects **F** **G**.

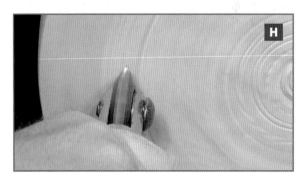

The star wheel is used here to create a textured line and define the outer edge of the decoration **H**.

Here we see the effects of the various tools in the textured surface of the wood **I**. Remember not to overdo the texturing.

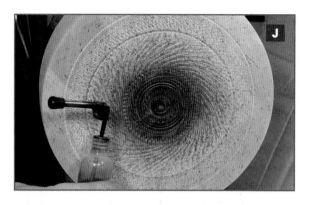

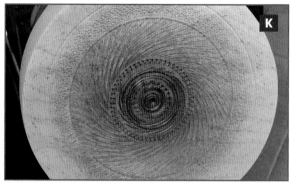

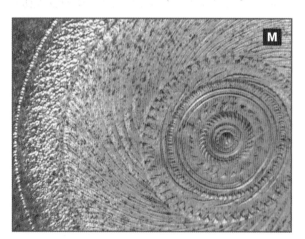

Colouring

5 Colour choice is personal. Again, experiment with the diffuser to blow colours onto a wood surface and discover for yourself what works. Always take notes of your experiments, as it is difficult to remember exactly what has been done to create great effects. Using spirit stain and diffuser blow red stain onto the centre of the rotating work **J**.

On the outside of this colour, and partly obscuring it, a yellow is sprayed **K**.

On the edge of the yellow orange is sprayed to 'pep' it up with black defining the outer edge and rim **L**.

Here we see the spirit stained surface **M**.

Now spread liming wax over the whole coloured, textured surface **N O**. It might seem wrong to cover the coloured surface, but have faith. When the liming wax is rubbed off using a cloth the effect is stunning **P**.

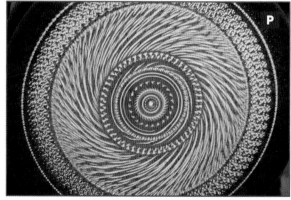

Looking close up at the coloured, textured surface we can see how the liming wax has filled the hollows but allows the coloured highlights to show through and actually accentuates them **Q**.

6 Remove the blank from the jam chuck. If hot melt glue 'tacks' have been used, place a chisel between the glue and the wood faceplate and tap with a mallet to break the glue's grip. Once all the 'tacks' have been loosened the blank will come free. To remove the glue from the blank, hold with the undecorated face towards you and press down on the glue, which will break free leaving little or no mark. The second blank may now be placed in the jam chuck so that its face may be textured and coloured in the same way.

Hollowing the interiors

7 First measure the thickness of the blanks and make a note. The thickness here is 1in (25mm). Fit the blank, textured face inward, into the jam chuck. Make sure that the face runs flat and true, then add hot melt glue 'tacks' to hold the blank in place. Lightly skim the surface of the blank, making sure that it is flat and true. On its outer edge mark, in pencil, a line ¼in (6mm) in from that edge **R**.

8 As the base of this vessel will be ¼in (6mm) thick, take this measurement away from the thickness of the blank. This will leave, in this case, ¾in (19mm). On a ⅜in- (9mm-) wide negative rake square end scraper tool **S**, use typist's correction fluid to mark a point ¾in (19mm) away from the cutting edge. Here the tool can be seen with its white depth mark **T**. A groove has been turned, on the inside of the marked pencil line, to the depth marked on the tool. A similar hollow has been turned to the same depth at the blank's centre. The central portion may now be turned away and if these two positions are joined it will ensure that a flat-bottomed ¼in- (6mm-) thick base is produced.

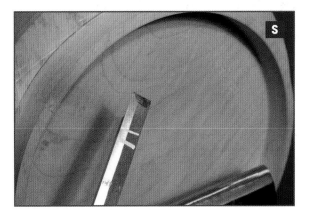

9 Remove the first blank and replace with the second, fixing it into the jam chuck, decorative face innermost, with hot melt glue 'tacks' as before. Hollow out the second blank but do not

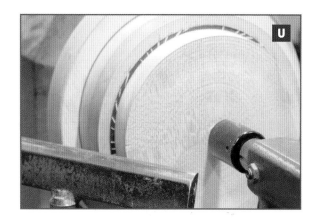

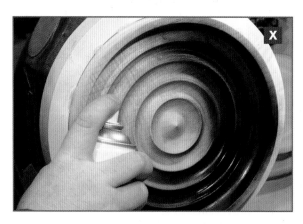

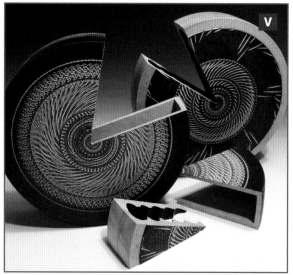

remove it from the jam chuck. Bring the first blank to the lathe. Apply white PVA glue to its edge and press it onto the blank held in the jam chuck. Bring up the tailstock, place a piece of wood against the textured surface, and then push the lathe centre into that protective wood, clamping the two blanks together. Make sure that the edges are flush before leaving the glue to set. Wipe off any excess glue U .

10 When the glue has set, switch on the lathe and clean up the edge. With careful application, colour may be added to the edge having masked the decorated face. Remove the piece from the jam chuck when satisfied and clean up any hot melt glue residue. Finally, take the piece to the bandsaw and cut a wedge to open the vessel V . Clean up the cut edge. Consider how you would like the vessel to sit, and then sand a flat to create a base in the appropriate position.

Thinking inside the box

It is not always necessary to turn the inside of the vessel perfectly flat. The inner surface can be turned with coves and beads W , and once these have been sanded they can be sprayed black using an ebonizing lacquer X Y .

If you want to be even more adventurous, you may like to turn a half profile on each side to produce a dramatic interior Z .

Cut-away view of
Inside the Box

By turning a profile on both interiors
you can create interesting silhouettes,
here a woman, and the attention is
taken from outside to inside the box.

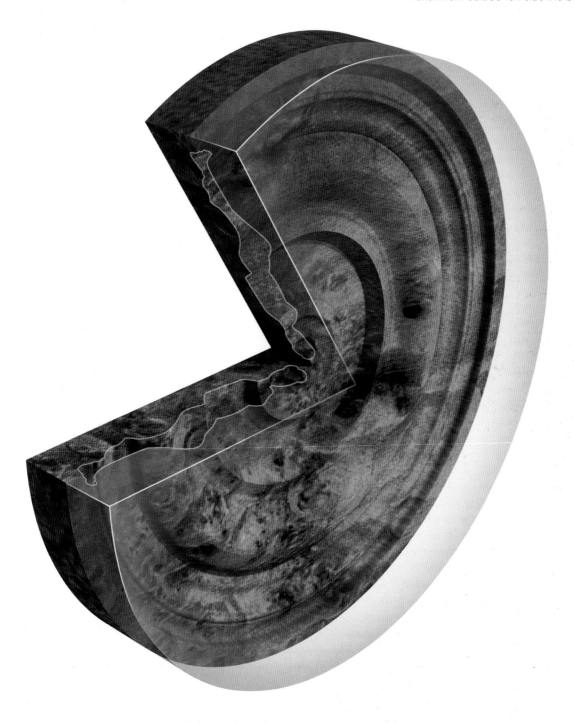

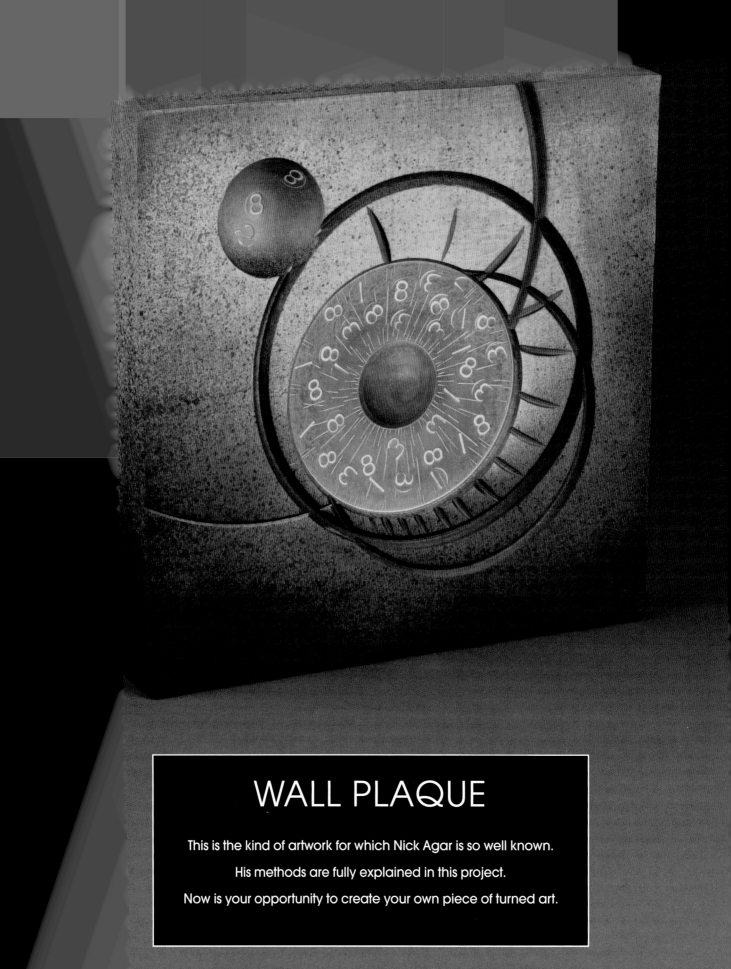

WALL PLAQUE

This is the kind of artwork for which Nick Agar is so well known.

His methods are fully explained in this project.

Now is your opportunity to create your own piece of turned art.

Art or craft?

When describing the production of this wall plaque, the approach to working, the techniques and the colouring method will all be discussed in detail but precise dimensions will not always be given, for this work is more of an art than a precise craft. The size of the plaque will depend upon the lathe that you will be using. The square blank must be able to rotate in the lathe without its corners touching the lathe bed, and remember to take into account the fact that the blank has to be set off-centre during the turning process.

Important safety considerations

If you feel that this project will take you outside your 'comfort zone' then don't do it. It may be wise to attend a course or reduce the size of the work so that you begin with a smaller piece to gain experience. Multiples of smaller plaques make a good collage. It is vital that you take the following points into account.

- The lathe must be firmly bolted to the floor.
- The lathe must have variable speed, for when turning out of centre the lathe speed needs to be adjusted to suit the 'throw' of the piece.
- Hold the turning tool using an underhand grip A . This will ensure that your arm and elbow are kept well back from the rotating work.
- Be fully aware that this rotating square blank forms a guillotine action as it passes the tool rest B . Keep your fingers away from this danger area. Remember the underhand grip.
- No loose clothing must be worn, and tie back long hair.
- Wear a peaked baseball cap throughout the turning of this off-centre work, for as your focus gets drawn to the work so too will your head

and face. If you get too close, your peaked hat will be hit and fly off – preventing your nose from following. It is all too easy to forget those sharp edges.
- Set the tool rest so that furthest (left hand) part is well past the corner of the spinning work C .
- Stand firm and stable at the lathe to prevent you stumbling into the rotating work.
- Regularly check the hot melt weld holding the work to the MDF backplate. If a gap should appear, make sure that it is reinforced with a little more hot melt glue.
- Nick has never felt the need to add counterbalancing weights to the off-centre work. It is better to reduce the speed of the lathe and work more steadily.
- Always rotate the lathe before starting work, to make sure that nothing catches.
- And finally, take care and enjoy producing what is sure to be a unique piece of work.

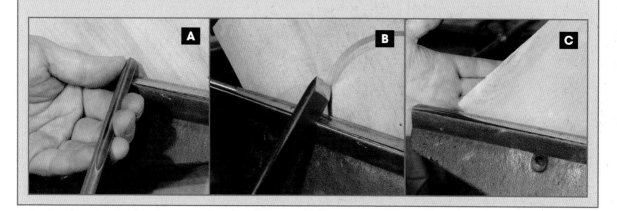

Tools and materials

In addition to the list of tools and materials shown on page 17 you will need the following:

- As the work is to be coloured, choose a square of plain, pale coloured hard wood such as sycamore, maple or a fruitwood. Here the piece is 12⅜in- (310mm-) square by 1¾in- (44mm-) thick sycamore
- For the backplate, a piece of ¾in- (18mm-) thick MDF that is ½in (12mm) smaller all round than the blank that you are using
- A 4in- (100mm-) diameter faceplate with at least 8 screw holes. These screw holes need to be countersunk on the underside (see step 3)
- For the V cut, a ¼in (6mm) superflute bowl gouge with a long fingernail grind with a bevel angle of about 55°

- A ¼in (6mm) gouge that has the base of the bevel rounded
- Number, letter or other decorative punches
- Coloured spirit stains and diffuser
- Liming wax and cloth
- An angle grinder with abrasive discs
- A poker pen

Preparation

1 Make sure that both faces and edges of the chosen blank are sanded clean. Choose the best face of the blank and place it face down on a bench. Set the MDF backplate on the blank, arranging it so that there is a ½in (12mm) space all round. In this case, for extra security, screw through just two diagonal corners to secure the MDF to the blank **D**. As you gain confidence in the hot melt weld this will not be necessary and will leave the back of the blank unmarked.

2 Using the hot melt glue gun, apply a hot melt weld all around the edge between the MDF and the blank. This weld should be quite thick but the glue should not be allowed to go under the MDF **E**. It is preferable to double glue the weld rather than leaving it light. Leave one corner unglued so that the blank may later be released by pushing a screwdriver between the MDF and the blank.

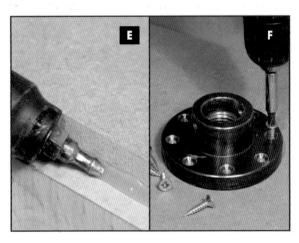

3 Next, centre the 4in (100mm) faceplate on the MDF backplate by eye and, for safety, screw it down using as many screws as possible **F**.

Because the MDF erupts around the area of the screw being driven in it is advisable to countersink the underside of the screw holes in the faceplate. The screws should fix firmly into the MDF but should not penetrate the blank. Fit the work onto the lathe and make sure that it clears the lathe bed, remembering that it will be off-set, so a large clearance is necessary. Clean the tool rest of any marks, cuts or hollows so that the tool will slide freely. Sharpen your tools.

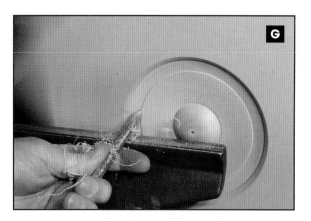

Turning the centre

4 The centre of the blank needs to be turned to draw the eye. Mark the centre of the work with a pencil and, using a suitable gouge turn a hollow with a dome at its centre **G** . The shape at the centre could easily be a spike instead of a bump. The choice is yours. Sand the surface smooth ready for texturing.

Decorating the centre

5 The centre may be decorated as described in the previous project, using texturing tools, but here number punches are used. Punch the decoration randomly and fill in gaps that become obvious, but don't overdo it **H** .

6 Using the poker pen, burn radiating lines into the central area **I** . These burnt lines are cut quite deep. If you do not have a poker pen then chiselled lines will work.

7 Spray a blue spirit stain onto the central area using a diffuser **J** while the work is rotating **K** . Alternatively a pump action spray may be used.

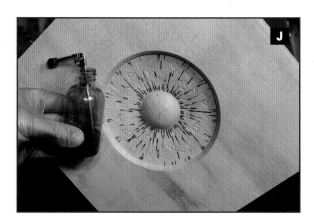

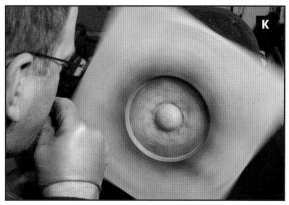

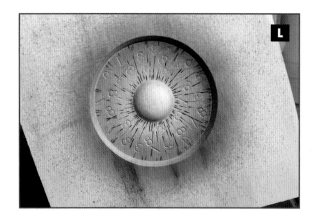

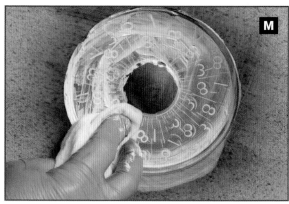

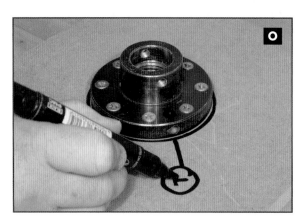

Leave the dome clean but do not worry about over-spraying the outer area **L** . The central dome area can now be sprayed with a red spirit stain.

8 Using vinyl gloves (as they will resist the alcohol base of the stain), rub liming wax into the central area leaving the dome clear. Now make a pad of cloth and hold it in your right hand. Use your left hand to hold the wrist. With the lathe running at a low speed, moving from the centre out, remove the liming wax **M** . This will leave a white residue in the indented areas **N** . Liming wax is not a filler – it is used to highlight shallow impressions. For deeper indents use a coloured filler.

Off-setting the centre of the plaque

9 Remove the blank from the lathe and lay it face down on a clean bench. Using a black marker pen, draw around the faceplate and mark a datum, number 1, opposite a clear feature on that faceplate **O** . Remove the faceplate and clean off the area around the screw holes. Reposition the faceplate about ⅝in (15mm) from the original position (this is not an exact science) and mark around the faceplate with a black marker pen, and mark datum point number 2 **P** . Screw the faceplate firmly into its new position and fit the blank onto the lathe.

Making the V cut

10 Rotate the lathe by hand to make sure nothing catches and decide where the first V cut will be placed. At its closest to the original

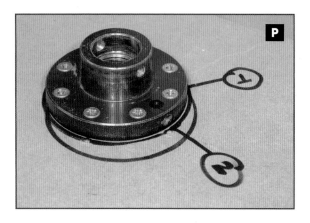

centre it should just skim the central hollow. Place a piece of tape on the tool rest to mark the start position **Q** **R** .

11 The tool used for these V cuts is a super flute bowl gouge with a long fingernail bevel ground to about 55°. While it is easier to turn at higher speeds, when the blank is off-set and out of balance it is better to turn at a lower speed. To hold the tool correctly, place the thumb of your right hand on top of the tool handle. This will apply pressure on the tool, forcing it down onto the tool rest **S** . Then place the thumb of your left hand behind the tool on the tool rest. This will prevent the tool from moving across. Note the underhand grip (for safety) and the four fingers actively holding the tool. Make sure the bevel of the tool rubs the wood as the cut progresses.

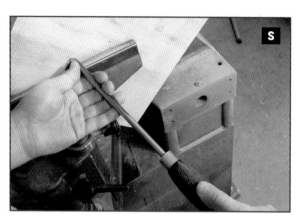

12 The initial cuts must be extremely light, slowly advancing in small increments **T** . Once the cut is about a bevel's width deep, halt. One side of the V will be cleanly cut, the other will be torn. Reverse the bevel direction and the cut about ⅟₁₆in (1mm) from that cut edge. The same cutting technique is used but this time the tool is drawn towards the turner **U** . Stop before the tool touches the left hand side of the V, which has been cleanly cut.

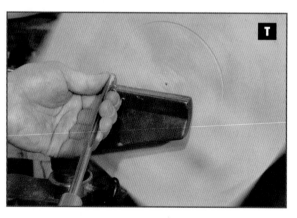

13 A small line of uncut wood remains at the base of the V. Either use a spindle gouge, with fingernail bevel, to remove this waste or, if you wish to accentuate the bottom of the V and remove the waste at the same time, use the long point of a skew **V** . Sometimes the small

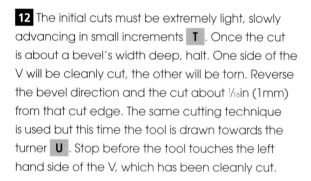

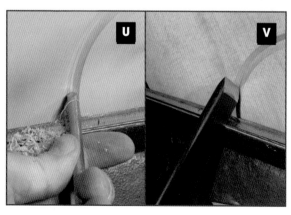

shaving at the base of the V can be removed with the thumb nail with the lathe rotated by hand. Do not overdo any accenting of the V base. It is worth practising this cut before beginning on an important piece.

Making the actual cuts on the plaque

14 Although the method of making this cut has been described here working from the left-hand side first and then completing the V from the right, it is best when working close to a decorated area to begin a cut that works away from that area. This will ensure that if a slip is made it will do less damage. So begin the cut at the tape marked position on the tool rest working from the right **W**. To begin with, do not make the cut too narrow. Start the cut that will complete the V, working from the left.

15 When the cut has been satisfactorily completed, use a disc of scrap wood to mask the central area **X**. If necessary, this cover can be held in place using the tailstock centre. When colouring the V rings do not be tempted to use a rainbow of colours but do break up a single colour. For example, here the dominant red has been tempered with blue. With the lathe switched off, spray red on one side and blue on the other while slowly rotating the lathe by hand **Y**. Note how the off-set V just skims the central hollow and the overspray of the surrounding area. Don't worry about the overspray – it will be dealt with later.

16 Remove the blank from the lathe and place it face down on a clean bench. Mark around the faceplate (if you have not already done this) and unscrew it from the backplate. Clean off any raised patches of MDF before relocating it on a new centre. Randomly reposition the faceplate quite a distance from the last setting, but check that the centre of the faceplate to the furthest corner will clear the lathe. Now, screw down the faceplate and mark, with a black marker pen, the new datum point 3 **Z**. These datum marks show the progression and will allow you to backtrack should you decide that an area needs to be re-cut. It's never exact, but it's the best you've got.

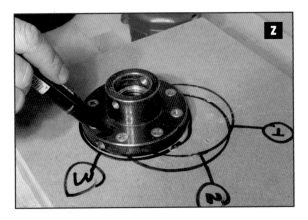

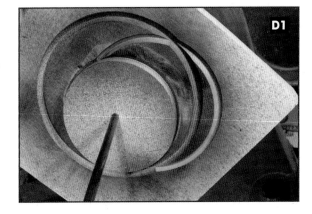

17 Replace the work on the lathe. On the face of the work locate a position for the second V cut. This will cross the outer area and the textured inner area but must avoid the domed centre. Mark the start position of this V cut, as before, using tape on the tool rest. Cut the V groove starting from the right or left, whichever you feel is more comfortable **A1**. Stop regularly to check the depth of the cut to avoid cutting into the textured area. Using the correct method to cut the V groove will create a clean junction where V cuts cross. It will also avoid break-out at this junction **B1**.

In this sequence of photographs **C1** **D1** **E1** we see the second cut waiting to be coloured with the central area masked so that the spirit stain may be sprayed to colour the V groove, the coloured groove, and the effect with the mask removed.

Useful information

- It is essential to make V cuts and not round coves. Coves cutting across coves are likely to break out.
- It is important that the tool should not bounce while cutting V grooves. If it does, slightly release the pressure on the tool and let the wood cut gently until the problem is corrected.
- If you make a mistake, relax and carry on; any of these pieces may be cut and reassembled to make an interesting collage. All is not lost.
- It is very useful to make a photo-diary as your work progresses. Often 'happy accidents' occur that, later, you may not remember.
- Knowing when to stop cannot be taught. You must decide for yourself.

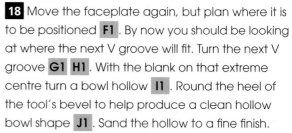

18 Move the faceplate again, but plan where it is to be positioned **F1**. By now you should be looking at where the next V groove will fit. Turn the next V groove **G1** **H1**. With the blank on that extreme centre turn a bowl hollow **I1**. Round the heel of the tool's bevel to help produce a clean hollow bowl shape **J1**. Sand the hollow to a fine finish.

19 We're now ready to spray more colour, so mask the central textured area again and spray orange spirit stain into the bowl hollow and the V groove. In the hollow, spray a black shadow on the 'wrong', unexpected, side of the bowl. This will cause the viewer to look twice at the finished piece. Now to carve some relief patterns. On a section between two intersecting V cuts, use an angle grinder (or carving chisel) with 24 or 36 grit disc **K1** to cut a series of lines. Note how these lines are closer together at the start and gradually move apart **L1**. Remember to wear eye protection. The over-sprayed areas can now be sanded clean using the angle grinder or sander **M1**.

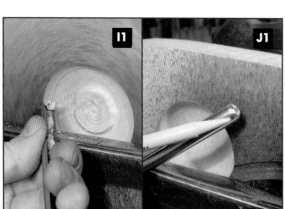

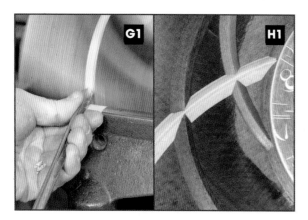

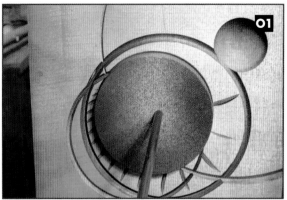

20 Now is the time to add colour to any V grooves that need improving and continue sanding. Work through the grades and move to a palm sander for a fine finish **N1**. The cleaned areas are now carefully coloured in a controlled manner. Mask the central textured area and spray with yellow and orange spirit stain **O1**. Darken the outer edges of the panel to provide a more dramatic effect **P1**.

If your wall plaque does not work out as you would hope, don't worry. Take two pieces of L-shaped black card **Q1** and use them to frame sections and find which areas look good **R1**. The piece may then be cut and 'rescued'. Hopefully, though, you'll get it right and it will look like this **S1**.

HORN

This project just about rounds off this whole turning adventure, bringing together the novel turning methods from the early part of this book and combining them with bronzing and decorative treatments from the latter part.

Tools and materials

In addition to the list of tools and materials shown on page 17 you will need:

- 4 pieces of planed oak or your choice of wood (the smallest diameter piece should be a burr)
  No.1: 9in (230mm) in diameter by ½in (12mm) thick
  No. 2: 9⁷⁄₁₆in (240mm) in diameter by ¹³⁄₁₆in (20mm) thick
  No. 3: 9⅞in (250mm) in diameter by 1in (25mm) thick
  No. 4: 6⅞in (175mm) in diameter by ⅝in (15mm) thick

- Bronzing materials as described in the Elephant, project (see page 98)
- Newspaper and PVA glue
- 8¾in (220mm) diameter wood faceplate fitted to metal faceplate
- ⅜in (9mm) gouge
- Cotton string, about ⅛in (3mm) diameter
- 8in- (200mm-) wide by ¼in- (6mm-) thick MDF for the stand

Preparation

1 Begin by fitting disc No. 1, 9in (230mm) in diameter by ½in (12mm) thick, centrally on the wood faceplate using newspaper and glue. Leave until the glue has set. Turn the edge true and square to the face, removing as little material as possible. Turn the piece to ⅜in (9mm) thick ensuring that the face is flat. Fit a shelf tool rest in the tool post and set it so that the square end tool cuts at centre height. Mark, using typist's correction fluid, a point on the square-end tool ¼in (6mm) away from the cutting edge.

2 Study the two diagrams on page 140 **1 2**, which show the dimensions of the hollows to be turned in the discs 1, 2 and 3, and the lines with their lettering to distinguish each. Mark, in pencil, an 8⅜in (210mm) diameter circle concentrically on the face of disc 1. This will be line A. Measure, towards the centre, ¹³⁄₃₂in (10mm) and mark a

second pencil circle. This will be line B. Using the square-end tool set on the shelf tool rest, turn a square-sided, flat-bottomed hollow ³⁄₁₆in (5mm) deep, between lines A and B **A**.

3 From line A, towards the outer edge, measure ³⁄₁₆in (5mm) and mark this as line D. Turn the outside of line D so that the outer edge is flat and square to the face of the work. From line B, towards the

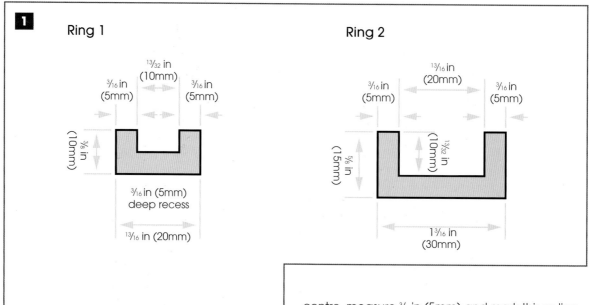

1

Ring 1

³⁄₁₆ in (5mm)
¹³⁄₃₂ in (10mm)
³⁄₁₆ in (5mm)

³⁄₈ in (10mm)

³⁄₁₆ in (5mm) deep recess

¹³⁄₁₆ in (20mm)

Ring 2

³⁄₁₆ in (5mm)
¹³⁄₁₆ in (20mm)
³⁄₁₆ in (5mm)

⁵⁄₈ in (15mm)

¹³⁄₃₂ in (10mm)

1³⁄₁₆ in (30mm)

Ring 3

³⁄₁₆ in (5mm)
1³⁄₁₆ in (30mm)
³⁄₁₆ in (5mm)

¹³⁄₁₆ in (20mm)

⁵⁄₈ in (15mm)

1⅝ in (40mm)

centre, measure ³⁄₁₆in (5mm) and mark this as line C. Using the square-end tool, turn on the centre side of line C until the faceplate is reached. Remember to widen the cut so that the tool is not 'grabbed'. Also make sure that the edge of line C is flat and square to the face of the work **B**.

B

2

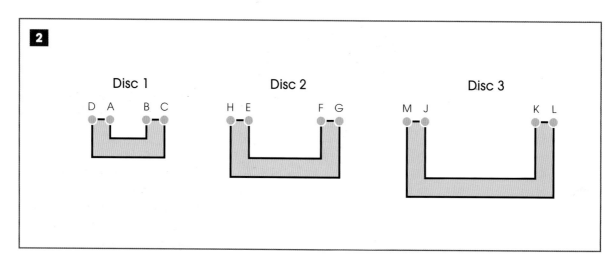

Disc 1

D A   B C

Disc 2

H E   F G

Disc 3

M J   K L

Cut-away view of the curved hollow squares

The three different-sized curved hollow square sections slide into one another. They are set in place, the positions marked, then glued into position to secure them.

4 When satisfied that (now) ring No.1 is complete, use a hammer and wood wedges to release it from the newspaper/glue joint on the faceplate **C**. Here we see the completed ring **D**. Clean away any newspaper and glue from the underside. Clearly mark the centre on the disc remaining fixed to the wood faceplate before removing it. This will enable it to be saved and later re-centred accurately if it is needed for another project.

5 Clean the wood faceplate before centrally fitting disc No. 2, using newspaper/glue, to the wood faceplate. Turn the face of disc No. 2 flat and true and to a thickness of ⅝in (15mm). Turn the edge round, removing as little material as possible. Measure ring No. 1 (about 8⅜in/210mm outer and 6¾in/170mm inner) and mark both its outer and inner diameters concentrically upon the face. It is important that the rings that are turned are measured and that those measurements are used. The outer pencil circle is line E and the inner pencil circle is line F.

6 Set the shelf tool rest in the tool post, again so that the square-end tool cuts at centre height. Clean off any existing depth marks from the tool and, using typist's correction fluid, mark a point ¹³⁄₃₂in (10mm) away from the cutting edge. Begin with a light cut on the centre side of line E and the non-centre side of line F. Join the two cuts to produce a shallow flat-bottomed trench **E**. Test ring No.1 in that cut area **F** adjusting the cut until it is a good fit. (Not too tight.) When satisfied, complete the cut between lines E and F until the

depth mark on the square-end tool is reached. Test ring No. 1 in the hollow. The edges of ring No. 1 *must* be slightly below the face of disc 2 G . Use a rule to make sure that this is the correct.

7 When satisfied, mark, in pencil, line H, which is ³⁄₁₆in (5mm) away from and on the outside of line E. Next measure ³⁄₁₆in (5mm) on the centre side of line F and mark pencil line G H . Turn on the outside of line H so that the edge is flat and square to the face of the work. Turn on the centre side of line G, widening the cut so the tool does not grab, until the faceplate is reached I . The edge of line G must be flat and square to the face of the work. Use a hammer and wood wedges to release ring No. 2 from the faceplate. Clean off any newspaper /glue from the underside of ring 2. Here we see rings No. 1 and 2 J . The first should fit flush inside the second.

8 Remove the centre waste from the faceplate as described earlier and clean the faceplate of any glued newspaper. Next, fit disc No. 3 centrally to the wood faceplate using newspaper/glue. Leave it to dry. Turn disc No. 3 to ¹³⁄₁₆in (20mm) thick with its face flat and true. Turn the edge of the disc clean, removing as little material as possible. Measure the outer and inner diameters of ring No. 2, approximately 8⅞in (225mm) outer and 6¼in (165mm) inner. Remember to measure the ring that you have turned and to use those measurements.

9 On the face of disc No. 3 mark, in pencil, line J (8⅞in/225mm approximate diameter). Next mark line K (6¼in/165mm approximate diameter). Remember to use your measurements in both cases. Clean off any existing depth marks from the square-end tool and, using typist's correction fluid, mark a point ⅝in (15mm) away from the cutting edge. Using the square-end tool set on the shelf tool rest, turn a test hollow between lines J and K. Test fit ring No. 2 into that hollow, adjusting until the fit is good. When satisfied, turn down between lines J and K to a depth of ⅝in (15mm), making sure that the edges are square to the face of the work and that the hollow is flat bottomed. Test ring No. 2 in the hollow K L , making sure that it is set below the top surface of disc No. 3.

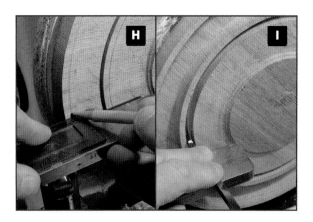

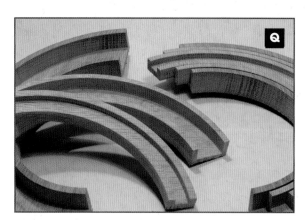

10 Measure and mark in pencil line M. This will be set ³⁄₁₆in (5mm) on the outside of line J. Measure and mark in pencil line L. This will be set ³⁄₁₆in (5mm) on the centre side of line K **M**. Using the square end tool turn on the outside of line M, making sure that the turned edge is flat and square to the face of the work. On the centre side of line L turn in, widening the cut so that the tool does not grab, until the faceplate is reached. Again make sure that the turned edge is flat and square to the face of the work **N**.

11 When satisfied, release ring No. 3 from the faceplate using thin wedges and a hammer **O**. All three rings are now complete and they will fit one within the other like nesting boxes **P**. Take the rings to the bandsaw and accurately cut across the diameter of each, cutting with the grain, to produce six half circles **Q**. Using black acrylic paint, paint the inside of ring No. 1 only **R**.

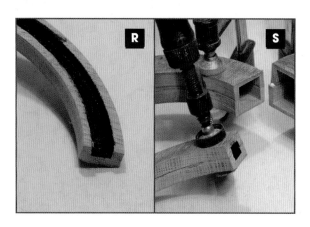

12 The half rings are now glued together accurately **S** to give three hollow rings **T**. It is important that glue squeezed out from the joints is cleaned off immediately, particularly from the inside. To do this, roll up a piece of newspaper and thread it through the hollow, pulling backwards and forwards.

13 Mark out the segments to be cut on each hollow half ring as shown in the diagrams below and overleaf **3** **4** **5** **6**.

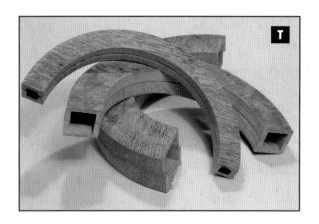

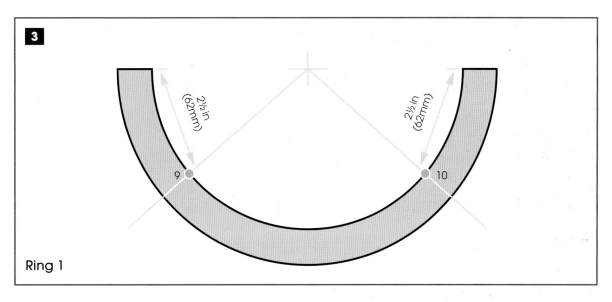

3

2½ in (62mm)

2½ in (62mm)

9

10

Ring 1

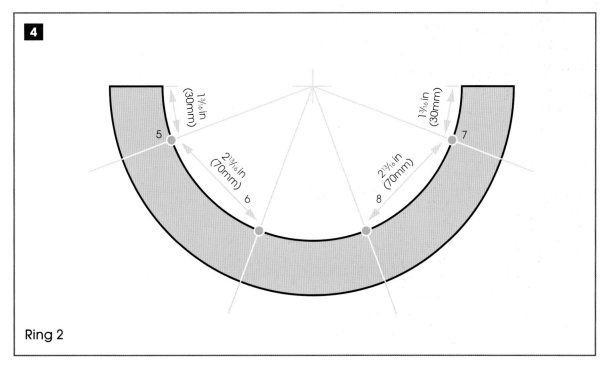

4

1³⁄₁₆ in (30mm)

1³⁄₁₆ in (30mm)

5

7

2¹³⁄₁₆ in (70mm)

2¹³⁄₁₆ in (70mm)

6

8

Ring 2

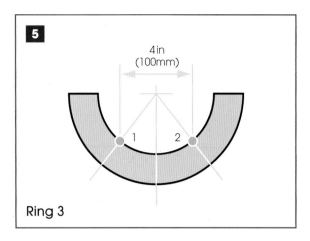

5

4 in
(100mm)

1   2

Ring 3

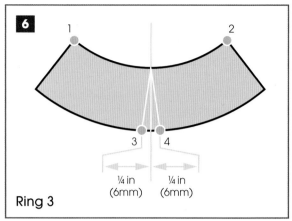

6

1   2

3   4

¼ in
(6mm)

¼ in
(6mm)

Ring 3

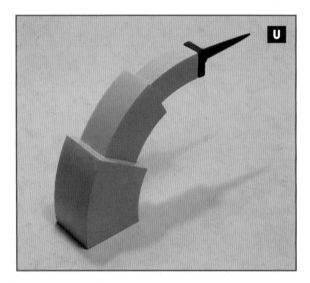

U

This 'Horn' form developed from an attempt to create some more lively 'Bendy buildings' (see page 157) **U** . When two of these building shapes were fitted together the form showed itself **V** . All the cuts that make the segments have to be radial cuts from the outside towards the perceived centre. One exception is the joining faces of ring No. 3. These are cut on a slight angle, as shown in the diagram on page 145 **4** , to open out the Horn form and make the curve less predictable.

14 Cut the segments on a bandsaw, but make sure it has a good sharp blade. Sand the cut ends of each segment on a sheet of abrasive paper

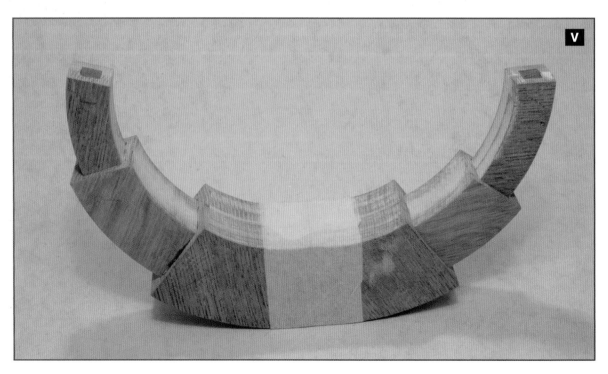

V

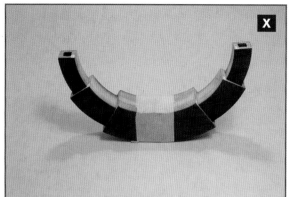

upon a flat surface W . When all the segments have been cut and sanded they may have their flat (not curved) surfaces charred and wire brushed to expose the grain, as described in the Kiwi project (see pages 73–75). The segments may now be glued together and held, while the glue sets, using masking tape. When the segments are firmly glued, the two halves may be butt jointed together using yellow glue X . Allow the glue to dry. Any gaps around the areas where one segment fits inside another may be carefully filled, then the piece is painted using black acrylic paint.

Wrapping the string

15 First decide upon the area to be wrapped with string. In this case it will be 1½in (40mm) long, so measure half that distance either side of the centre join line. Mark using a white crayon. Using yellow glue, fix the string at one mark on the underside of the form. Hold it in place while the glue sets using a clamp Y .

16 When the glue has dried, remove the clamp and carefully wrap the string tightly around the form. When the string reaches the second mark, underneath, apply some more glue and clamp the string in place Z . When the glue has dried, use a scalpel, or a sharp knife, to trim the ends of the string. Apply glue along the underside of the string to lock it all in place A1 . When this glue has dried the string may be painted black. As the string is cotton it will absorb the colour, particularly if the paint is thinned.

The central disc

17 The central disc, No.4, is 6⅞in- (175mm-) diameter by ⅝in- (15mm-) thick burr oak. It is important to use a burr as this will provide a randomly pitted surface that will enhance the bronzing techniques applied to that surface. Although here the turned disc is held by a vacuum chuck, as an alternative it can be fixed to a wood faceplate using newspaper and glue. The piece is turned with a 2in- (50mm-) diameter shallow dome at the centre and a series of incised lines around the outer edge. To relieve the flat surface between the dome and the incised lines a series of hollows have been cut with carving burrs and chisels. The whole surface of the wood is charred then using a stiff scrubbing brush the burnt material is brushed away **B1**.

18 Spray the whole disc with an acrylic ebonizing spray **C1**. Then paint the centre dome with gold acrylic paint **D1**. Now take a very small amount of gold Goldfinger **E1**, rub it between thumb and

forefinger **F1** and then *lightly* rub over the surface of the disc to highlight the texture **G1**. Here we see the finished disc **H1**.

Making the stand

19 The stand is made from ¼in (6mm) MDF. The front and back are cut 12in (300mm) long with a 2¹³⁄₁₆in (70mm) base tapering to a 1⅝in (40mm) top, tapering equally on both sides. The two sides are cut 12in (300mm) long and 1⅝in (40mm) wide. The pieces are butt jointed together using yellow glue and held in place using masking tape while the glue sets. The face is textured with random slash cuts, and three panels are carved and textured to provide relief. When fully sanded and cleaned up the stand is sprayed with an acrylic ebonizing spray. The three textured panels are picked out with gold Goldfinger **I1**.

20 To raise the central disc up off the string wrapped area, a small saddle of MDF is cut, textured, ebonized and gilded **J1**. And here we see the finished piece **K1**.

THE GALLERY

This book should not finish when the last page is closed.
We hope that you will be sufficiently stimulated to see the
possibility of developing new ideas and understand that
woodturned pieces do not necessarily have be round.

Kingwood elephant vessel

7³/₁₆in (180mm) long by 3³/₈in (85mm) wide by 1³/₈in (35mm) thick

The real advantage of turning pieces using the methods described in this book is clearly shown in this vessel. A small piece of kingwood is transformed into a useful, shapely and saleable hollow vessel which is over 6³/₈in (160mm) high.

Unlocking my potential

27in (685.8mm) diameter by 2¹³⁄₁₆in (70mm) thick
End-grain multiple-centred turned and carved
jarrah sculpture with old metal keys inserted.

8in (200mm) high

This sculptural piece is very closely based upon a ceramic
piece by Robert L. Wood. I liked it so much I decided to
make it in wood. In turn it led onto a second similar piece,
then helped with the 'Bendy buildings' (see page 157) and
further transformed into the piece shown in the Horn project.

vessel with 3D spots

4½in (115mm) high

I do like the textural effect that 3D paint spots have
upon a surface. When colour is removed, the effect can
be quite striking. I did not know what to do about the lid.
Should it also have texture? When I fitted the lid and
saw the contrast between the stark white of the body
and the beige of the lid I realized that it needed
nothing more.

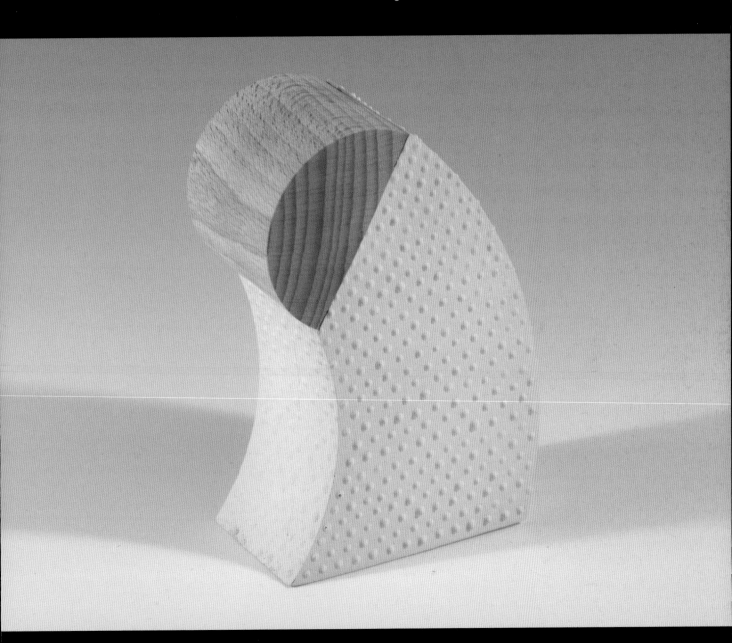

Bendy buildings

6in (150mm) and 5in (125mm) high

As soon as these sweeping forms were capped with spiked lids they had to be buildings bent double in a storm. A little work on the computer produced a series of curved windows that was far more precise than painting or airbrushing could produce. Playful ideas.

Mirror-image iguana

4½in (115mm) high

Nick was playing with a computer programme
that mirrored objects, so we made one of the
pieces created by the programme. If you are
ever stuck for ideas or inspiration, try holding a
mirror on part of your work and see if you find
the effect of value.

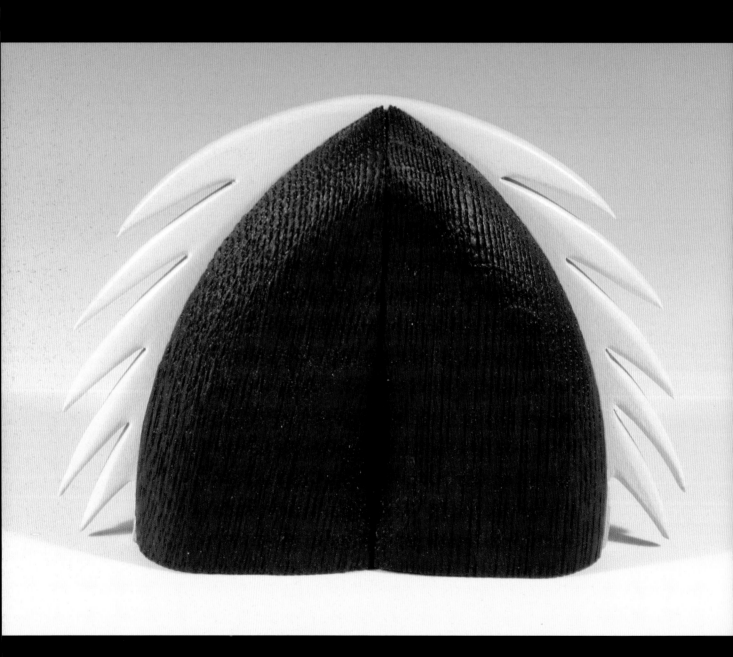

Reclining nude

15 inches (380mm) long

A single Y cross-section ring has been cut into quarters, and then those pieces have been twisted upon one another and glued in place. A Y cross-section spindleis then turned, split and used as end caps to complete this sinuous form. Yes, it's a bubble-gum pink, but the form just felt right with that colour. This form has only two sides.

Contorted Y form

11 inches (275mm) long

Here the yew Y cross-section turned ring is cut into
four segments and the parts are twisted before
being re-assembled. The ends are capped with
split halves of a Y cross-section spindle.

Mixed forms

Height 12in (300mm). Largest
cross-section 3in (75mm)
by 1¾in (45mm). Smallest
cross-section 1in (25mm)
by 1¾in (45mm)

Hybrid forms can be made
by fitting two different vessels
together. As long as the
cross-section at the point of
joining is the same, a variety of
hybrid forms can be produced.
Here a part of a 'Chinese' vessel
(see page 42) is joined to an
'Elephant' form (see page 94).
To ensure that the end cross-
sections match, as long as they
are of the same thickness, just
measure along the form(s) until
each has the same length of
side and then they can be
glued together.

Crazy paving

Height 12in (300mm)

Sweeping curved sections have been marked
with a poker pen and then those sections have
been airbrushed with colour.

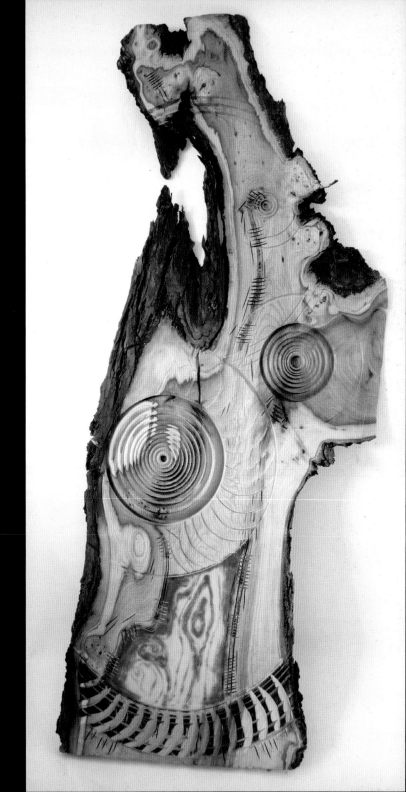

Cornish elm
wall sculpture

5ft (1500mm) high by
17¾in (450mm) wide by 1½in
(38mm) thick

This elm piece was multi-centre
turned, carved with an angle
grinder, scorched and lime
waxed. It has a Danish oil finish.

Jarrah sculpture

22⅝in (575mm) in diameter
by 6in (150mm) deep
This is Jarrah burr that has been turned
on both sides, carved and coppered.

Bits and bobs
wall sculpture

17½in (450mm) tall by 43in (1100mm)
long by 3in (75mm) deep

This is made up as a collage of parts from
demonstration work using ash and sycamore
with spirit stains, lime wax and acrylic lacquer.

Free-standing, bark-edged, sculpture

4in (100mm) by 15¾in (400mm) by 2in (50mm) thick

This ash piece was multi-centre turned, coloured with spirit stain and finished with acrylic lacquer.

Suppliers

Many of the suppliers listed have a wide range of woodturning tools and equipment. Here, we have only listed specific items purchased from each one.

Ashley Iles (Edge tools) Ltd.
www.ashleyiles.turningtools.co.uk
+44 (0)1790 76337
High Speed Steel blanks

Axminster Tool Centre
www.axminster.co.uk
+44 (0)800 371822
Arbortech wood carver

Chestnut Products
www.chestnutproducts.co.uk
+44 (0)1473 425878
Stains and polishes

Crown Hand Tools
www.crownhandtools.co.uk
+44 (0)1142 612300
Texturing tools

Daler-Rowney
www.daler-rowney.com
+44 (0)1344 461000 (head office)
+1 609 655 5252 (Daler-Rowney USA)
+33 (0)1 42 42 02 00 (Daler-Rowney Europe)
Goldfinger range of metallic waxes

Golden Artist Colors
www.goldenpaints.com
+1 607 847 6154 NY
Airbrush colours and texture paint

Graphics Direct
www.graphicsdirect.co.uk
+44 (0)1423 359730
Airbrush equipment and colours

Henry Taylor Tools Limited
www.henrytaylortools.co.uk
+44 (0)114 234 0282
+44 (0)114 234 0321
Woodturning tools

Jet Tools
www.jettools.com
+41 44806 4748
Lathes

John Bradford timber
+44 (0)1404 814533
Timber supplies

Middlesex University Teaching Resources
www.mutr.co.uk
+44 (0)1992 716052
Rare earth magnets and fascinating stuff

Phil irons Woodturning
www.philirons.com
+44 (0)1789 204052
Woodturning chucks

Robert Sorby
www.robert-sorby.co.uk
+44 (0)114 225 0700
Woodturning tools

Rolsten Timber
+44 (0)1886 833612
Timber supplies

Torn y Fusta
www.tornyfusta.com
+34 971 906862
Turning equipment

Verktoy As
www.verktoyas.no
+47 518 86800
Mechanical carving tools and blades

Vicmarc
www.vicmarc.com
+61 (0)7 3284 3103
Lathes

Wood Carvers Supply, Inc.
www.woodcarverssupply.com
+1 800 284 6229
Everything for the woodcarver

Acknowledgements

David Springett would like to thank the following people who helped in the preparation of this book: Dan Crowe, Tony Iles of Ashley Iles (Edge Tools), Neil Terry, Nick and Minggu Siarbawa, Christine Springett, Robin Springett and Ian Whitelaw (Editor). David would particularly like to thank Dominique Page (Senior Project Editor) and Chloë Alexander (Designer) for the thoughtful way they produced this stylish book.

Picture credits
All photographs by Nick Agar and David Springett except for the following:

Anthony Bailey/GMC: 1; 2; 5; 6; 7; 13 top left; 24; 32; 33; 34; 35 top; 42; 43 top; 54; 55 top; 62; 63 top; 68; 69 top; 72; 73 top; 76; 76 bottom; 86; 87 top; 94; 95 top; 104; 105 top; 110; 111 top; 120; 121 top; 128; 130 top; 138; 139 top.

Nick Agar would like to thank the following people who have supported him and kept him going: the late Bert Marsh, Stuart and Lynda Mortimer, Barry S, Barney the boat builder, Ted and Hils, my family, Sheila and Steve, Les and Liz Thorne, Chris and Ali, Keith and Bron S, Jaques and Minda Vesery, Odd Eric and Judith, Shaun S, David, Tom and Maurice, Paul and Mon, Henry Taylor Tools, Axminster Power Tools, The AAW, The AWGB, The AWSA, The Worshipful Company of Turners, my many customers and collectors without whom I would not have come so far, and Chloë for her patience.

Finally we would like to thank all our woodturning friends around the world who have made our woodturning journey such a pleasure.

About the authors

Nick Agar

Woodturning artist Nick Agar's large-scale, multi-textured wood sculptures, created at his riverside studio in Devon, England, have earned him a reputation for producing highly individual, beautifully crafted art.

'I like to push the boundaries of woodturning and take inspiration from the natural world around me, from architecture, ceramics and cultures worldwide. I feel a strong connection with the ancient civilizations and often use this to influence my work.'

In 2009 Nick was awarded a bursary by The Worshipful Company of Turners, based in London, to further explore his craft. Nick is on the Register of Professional turners (RPT) and is a member of AWGB, WAWA and AAW.

In addition to exhibiting widely and appearing at international conferences, both as a demonstrator and a judge, Nick is in constant demand for commissions from both collectors and galleries. His wide range of clients includes HRH Prince Charles, Prince of Wales, and Royal jewellers, Aspreys. He and his work have also featured on television programmes in the UK.

In recent years Nick has been invited across the globe to share his skills and ideas; in 2009 alone he visited Australia, South Africa, Canada, Belgium, Norway, France and Ireland to lecture and demonstrate.

Nick runs woodturning courses in Devon, England. Please visit the website www.turningintoart.com for more details.

David Springett

A former woodwork teacher, David Springett has been a professional woodturner for over 30 years. Specialising, at first, in lace bobbins, he became increasingly attracted to more experimental work such as the seemingly impossible pieces described in his first book, published by GMC Publications, *Woodturning Wizardry*, which was also revised and expanded. He has demonstrated his woodturning techniques throughout the UK and USA, Canada, Germany, Israel and Ireland.

In 2005 he was asked to present a paper detailing his work on woodturned Streptohedrons, to the Bridges Maths. Symposium in London. In 2007 he was invited to exhibit some of his turned sculptural pieces at Intersculpt 2007, which was held at the École Nationale Supérieure d'Arts et Métiers in Paris.

David is on the Register of Professional Turners (RPT) and is a member of the SOT, AWGB and AAW. David has three other books published by GMC Publications.

Index

Titles of projects and objects in Gallery are printed in **bold**.

To place an order, or to request a catalogue, contact:
GMC Publications
Castle Place, 166 High Street, Lewes, East Sussex, BN7 1XU
United Kingdom
Tel: +44 (0)1273 488005 Fax: +44 (0)1273 402866
Website: www.gmcbooks.com
Orders by credit card are accepted